Using Schema Play Theory to Advocate for Free Play in Early Childhood

Using Schema Play Theory to Advocate for Free Play in Early Childhood

Heather Bernt-Santy

Foreword by Lisa Murphy

Teachers College Press
Teachers College, Columbia University

Published by Teachers College Press,® 1234 Amsterdam Avenue, New York, NY 10027

Copyright © 2025 by Teachers College, Columbia University

Front cover design by Peter Donahue. Photo by Stock Color / iStock by Getty Images.

Library of Congress Cataloging-in-Publication Data is available at loc.gov

ISBN 978-0-8077-8724-3 (paper)
ISBN 978-0-8077-8725-0 (hardcover)
ISBN 978-0-8077-8317-7 (ebook)

Printed on acid-free paper
Manufactured in the United States of America

I dedicate this book to all the children who have allowed me into their play, and to all the families who have trusted me with their children. What a gift you have given me.

Contents

Foreword

In Chapter VI of *Alice's Adventures in Wonderland*, while standing unnoticed outside the house of the Duchess, Alice observes the Fish Footman deliver an invitation to play croquet, which is in turn received by the Frog Footman. We read that she *felt very curious to know what it was all about*. But while Alice creeps further away to behold the goings on, Heather Bernt-Santy engages a reader's curiosity to come closer and fall down the rabbit hole of schema play so as to understand the important role it plays in advocating for free play in early childhood.

As I read my advance copy in preparation for writing this foreword, the word that kept emerging for me was *curiosity*. I immediately called Heather and told her that we had been on the same wavelength, even though we hadn't discussed it. I had recently outlined a new article where I posit that when we remain curious about our work, we become more willing to do what needs to be done in order to feel confident when we talk with the crowds of people who, in the misinformed name of "readiness," stand in the way of free play in early childhood. In this new book, Heather shows readers how schema play is developmentally appropriate play, which is the only true form of readiness we need to be worried about.

When I first met Heather, my knowledge of "schema" was the same, as she will tell you in the forthcoming pages, as that of her graduate professor—limited to the few paragraphs one might read within the Piaget chapter of any college-level education or psychology textbook.

Chris Athey who? How little did I know.

I am quite thankful to have found myself in Heather's orbit on a pretty regular basis as she started and completed her master's degree and, as happens when people share thoughts and ideas and ponderings over coffee and wine and in hallways at conferences and on podcasts, I was in a unique position to observe the *deepening* of her understanding of a topic she continues to be so passionate about. Heather was fine-tuning a graduate-level thesis argument and I, like many a novice apprentice, was finding a beginning and an inspiration in the notes she left scattered on the floor.

In the following pages Heather calls upon her own contribution to schema play scholarship, the foundational work of Chris Athey, and, being the academic that she is, the input of many additional authors, researchers, and educators. Readers are invited to join a pedagogical tea party with colleagues who add richness and depth to her original content; yet even with the inclusion of a strong supporting cast, it is Heather's voice we hear throughout.

How helpful it has been, via Heather's inspiration, to learn more about schema play and to now have a theoretical context not only to apply within my own practice, but also to share with others. Even with my entry-level understanding, I have been able to reassure both educators and parents that when children spin on their bottoms during story time, dump the basket of warm laundry on their heads, squeeze themselves into the cupboard with the pots and pans, or stuff all of the action figures into a teeny tiny backpack, the children are *not* being naughty; they are playfully, and appropriately, exploring their environments. Using realistic examples of what might initially appear to be tiresome, meaningless, repetitive behaviors, Heather encourages a shift in understanding by inviting adults to now see these same actions through the schema play lens she skillfully brings into focus.

While I had a jolly bit of fun analyzing *Alice's Adventures in Wonderland* through a schema play lens, Heather takes the theory off the bookshelf and applies it to scenarios that readers see each and every day. Readers will be encouraged to become so curious about the children in their care that they will feel compelled to transform, at their core, how they see their own Lizzie, George, Alejandro, Max, Millie, Caleb, Link, Ann, and Bert, replacing notions of child misbehavior and naughtiness with a broader lens of childhood curiosity and deep investigation.

So come join Heather at a tea party where like-minded, slightly mad colleagues are working tirelessly to bring the never-ending caucus race of readiness to a halt, shed the play modifiers, and embrace free play for free play's sake. The conversation around the table has been one of cabbages and kings for all too long, and it is high time we acknowledge that the Queen of Hearts and her crowd of naysayers are nothing but a pack of cards. The body of work that Heather has assembled on how to use schema play to advocate for free play in early childhood might be what finally allows us to start talking about other things. For this I remain not only curious, but entirely grateful.

—Lisa Murphy
Orlando, Florida
February 2025

Acknowledgments

Writing this book was a terrifying and joyful thing to do, and I am so grateful for those who were with me through the process.

I want to thank all of the children who have played in my presence and inspired my curiosity and led me down this path.

Thank you, Curtis, for reminding me that my dreams of *how* I would one day be a writer are just as worthwhile as the product of all the writing and that my process did not need to be like other people's processes.

Thank you, Josie, for reminding me that even when it was really hard, I was going to write a great book that might change lives.

Thank you, Steve, for being my constant cheerleader and for telling literally everyone who mentioned me that I was working on a book and you were so proud of me. And for your patience during the bajillion times I said, "I really need to get some writing done," and then didn't.

Thank you to Jeff Johnson and Lisa Murphy for inviting me to be a guest on *The Child Care Bar and Grill* in 2016. And Jeff, even though when I told you I wanted to write a book you said, "No one reads anymore. But I'll help you start a podcast," I hope you'll read this book.

Thank you to Stacy Benge for the rad playlists.

Thank you to Dr. Jessica Sturm for meeting me every week for our #WritingPlayGroup.

Thank you to my podcast *Nerd Coven*: Tiffany Pearsall, Bethany Corrie, Lizz Nolasco, Richard Cohen, Mike Huber, Carol Garboden Murray, Kisa Marx, and Stacy Benge for endless chat group encouragement, for letting me text you when I hated my ideas and couldn't find my writing rhythm. I'm so lucky.

CHAPTER 1

What Is Schema Play Theory?

When the time came for me to select the topic of my thesis project in my graduate program, I knew it would be related to play. I'd spent the few years leading up to my graduate work in professional evolution. I'd always instinctively focused on relationships, care, and following the child in my practices with children, but I also talked a lot about *teaching*. I had at least one foot fully in the camp that said, "We can't just let them *play;* if we want to be seen as professionals, we have to *teach.*"

After 2 decades of working from that framework, my mind began to change in a way that more closely matched my intuition. I had been reading more about free play, listening to podcasts about free play, and finally, I placed both feet firmly in the camp that said, "to play freely is a child's human right."

As I thought about which element of play would be the best fit for my thesis, I remembered that my friend and colleague Tiffany Pearsall had sent me some links about something called "schema play" a year before. I had ignored it. I assumed "schema play" was another in a long line of buzzwords the early childhood profession loves to grab onto, and then to let go of when the next trend comes along. But now that I needed a unique research focus, I revisited the links she had sent and decided I would write about schema play theory. By this time, I had started to notice play schemas with the children in my classrooms.

As part of the thesis process, each student had to submit a topic and specific focus to a professor. In my pitch, I wrote that I had been learning about schema play, which was a new topic for me. I described how most of the preliminary research I had done indicated that this theory was well known in places like the United Kingdom, Canada, Australia, and New Zealand, but that resources from the United States were virtually nonexistent. My professor challenged this. Surely, she said, *everyone* who studied education or psychology in the United States knew about *schemas*. She didn't understand my position.

She was thinking of Jean Piaget. *I* was thinking of Chris Athey.

JEAN PIAGET

My professor was right—Swiss psychologist Jean Piaget's work is included in just about every education textbook used by students in the United States. His work centered on how children build knowledge and gain an understanding of the world around them. He highlighted the importance of a child's active engagement with their environment and introduced the idea that children utilize *schemas* (a mental image or pattern of action to organize information and in turn interpret future experiences) in their active learning process. He described a process of disequilibrium, accommodation, and assimilation as children encountered the world around them. Here's an example of the process Piaget posited:

> Two-year-old Cassius has a pet cat at home. One day while on a walk with his dads, he sees a woman approaching with a dog on a leash. The animal he sees walks on four legs and has fur. This fits his "pet" schema. The information in this current schema is that pets have fur and four legs. So far, he can comfortably apply his existing schema to this new experience.
>
> As they get closer to the woman, the dog barks. In Cassius's pet schema, which has developed from his life experiences so far, pets meow! This new information does not fit his existing schema. He enters a state Piaget called "disequilibrium." Disequilibrium causes discomfort and confusion, and Cassius's brain needs more information and more experiences to accommodate this new data.
>
> As he encounters more information through more experiences with animals, he will create new schemas like dog, cat, zoo animal, farm animal, animals I can approach, animals that I should leave alone. If given the opportunity to continue to explore his world, he will continue to change schemas to explain new input.

My professor was also experiencing disequilibrium. Her schema about . . . well, *schema*, was pushed into disequilibrium when I introduced a different theory that used similar language. The word "schema" fit an existing schema. The name Chris Athey did not.

CHRIS ATHEY

The idea of schema learning may have originated with the work of Jean Piaget, but it has been extended by the research of Chris Athey, who identified specific *play schemas* over several years of observing children.

As principal lecturer in education at Roehampton Institute of Higher Education in London, Chris Athey led the Froebel Early Education Project from 1973 to 1978. Athey and her team observed and analyzed children to better understand the development of children's thinking.

The team analyzed more than 5,000 observations of 20 children ages 2 to 5 years old. Children attended 3-hour daily sessions over the course of 2 years. The most important findings of the project were the prevalence of "schemas," or patterns of behavior and thinking in young children's play. Athey identified over 40 of these patterns of behavior, but the list is often simplified into the following categories:

- Dynamic vertical
- Dynamic back and forth
- Circular direction and rotation
- Going over, under, or on top
- Going around a boundary
- Enveloping and containing
- Going through a boundary
- Thought

In these schemas, she was able to see intention and meaning in behavior that is often seen as aimlessly "flitting" from object to object. Where some people would have labeled this flitting behavior as a lack of ability to play purposefully, to engage and pay attention to activities, or as disruptive, Athey's schema view assigned constructivist learning to these actions and posited that we could see "threads of children's thinking" by noticing their explorations more deeply and respectfully.

These findings support Piaget's theory of mental schemas as children construct their learning. Piaget believed that when young children repeat actions, "they are able to transfer their ideas into similar situations or generalize them into early concepts about the world around them" (Grimmer, 2017, p. 12). What Chris Athey saw in her research was children acting out Piaget's theory, and she was able to name specific repetitions she saw. As a child repeatedly explored rotation with a variety of materials over and over, for example, she saw them testing to see if what they expected to happen based on previous experience would happen again, and move through the assimilation and accommodation process. Piaget's ideas and Athey's observations have been validated by current neuroscience—a white paper developed by the LEGO Foundation (Zosh et al., 2017) on neuroscience and learning through play. Identified being "iterative" as a key characteristic of experiences that help children grow and thrive (p. 25).

Subsequent works around Athey's theory have adopted different labels for these schemas:

- Transforming
- Trajectory
- Transporting
- Rotation and circularity
- Enclosing and enveloping
- Connecting and disconnecting
- Positioning and ordering
- Orientation and perspective

These are the labels this book will use to describe the repeated patterns Athey's team found in their analysis of children's play. While this chapter will offer brief introductions, each schema will be discussed fully in the coming chapters.

Transforming

Red and blue playdough becomes purplish brown. The glob of tempera paint at the end of a brush becomes a smooth shiny path on the easel paper. Two 3-year-olds become a cat and its owner. A toy cash register scanner becomes the infrared thermometer that scans each child and family as they enter the program each morning. A 2-year-old switches from using his typical voice to making louder noises. These children are exploring the *transforming* schema as they use materials (including themselves) to explore how shape, color, consistency, and other characteristics can be changed.

Trajectory

When children drop food from their high chair, throw or kick balls, roll trucks and cars across surfaces or down inclines, push swings, jump off of the bottom of the slide, pull each other in wagons, or change the flow of water from a faucet, they may be experimenting with a *trajectory* schema. During these experiences, they discover new information about horizontal, diagonal, and vertical movements of objects and of themselves. In the trajectory schema, children explore and experiment with how objects and people move through space, and how their own actions can influence these movements.

Transporting

Two-year-old Lizzie always seems to have full hands as she goes through her day in her child care classroom. Five-year-old Michael works determinedly to hold three scooter boards together and move the objects he's loaded on top of each one around the room. Three-year-old Alejandro walks away from the sand table with a measuring cup full of sand. One-year-old Lucy takes baskets off the shelves in her classroom and empties them onto the floor without interacting with the materials. These are examples of the *transporting* schema, where we see children picking things up, moving them around the room, putting them down, or dumping them out. Noticing and supporting this play schema demands that adults shift away from their *product* orientation ("Why does she just move the blocks but never builds with them?") to the child's *process* orientation ("I am enjoying and learning from the process of just moving things around.")

Rotation and Circularity

In the *rotation and circularity* play schema, children are experimenting with things that turn—wheels, balls, themselves—and with curved lines or circles. A child who carries a cardboard tube to look through may be intrigued by how seeing things through a circle changes what he notices. The child who spends as much time as she can pouring water over a water wheel in the sensory table may be more interested in the motion of the wheel and the way the speed of the turning varies than in the water itself. When three 4-year-old boys take the paint rollers and begin to paint across the smocks they are wearing, they may be simply having fun using the rolling motion on a new surface and with a different viewpoint rather than "misbehaving."

Enclosing and Enveloping

Four-year-old George was deeply engaged in the *enclosing and enveloping* play schema. As I shared information with his mother about the play I was noticing (crunching paper into "wads" and putting them in drawers around the classroom, building doors that can open and close in all of the structures he constructed with magnetic plastic tiles, creating block enclosures for plastic animals, building pillow forts, hiding counting bears inside "blobs" of flubber or playdough, and preferring to work under tables rather than sitting at them), it helped her understand that this was not just "weird," meaningless play. She was excited to hear and see the ways that George explored and the things he might be learning as he enclosed and enveloped.

Connecting and Disconnecting

Children who are working within a *connecting and disconnecting* play schema do just what the name implies—they join things together and take them apart in a variety of ways. Building block towers, using tape or staples in the writing area, joining train tracks, and playing chase games are all examples of the ways we see this schema present itself in children's play. We may also see it in ways that are more difficult to value—the "disconnecting" element of this schema often presents as knocking down block towers, scattering toys from tabletops, or tearing paper. As will be discussed throughout this book, understanding schema play theory not only helps us to understand children's actions and to support their play, it also offers a useful prompt to be more curious about actions that might typically be considered "misbehavior."

Positioning and Ordering

Some children become interested in lining up toys like cars or animals in a row, sorting materials by different characteristics, and creating patterns. This is the *positioning and ordering* play schema. This schema is often discouraged by adults who misunderstand the child's purpose or intention (or who misunderstand *play*). Some adults will immediately become concerned about a young child lining up toys repetitively because they have learned that this might be an indicator of autism, and so they discourage or try to teach the child out of this play schema. A key element that I really appreciate about the theory of schema play is that it gives us a different perspective on play that might otherwise be labeled as "nonfunctional" or lead to behavioral goals focused on stopping this way of playing. It's important to note that positioning and ordering play is not always a sign of neurodivergence. It's also important to note that it is a disservice to autistic children when their way of playing is seen as meaningless or in need of intervention.

Orientation and Perspective

As adults, it may not make much sense to explore the world in the ways that children engaging in an *orientation and perspective* play schema often do—climbing furniture or other structures, sitting upside down, hanging from bars, crawling under tables, or looking through holes—but these young children are focused on the *process* of trying things in different ways. Each time a child engages in one of the actions listed above, they gain new data about the world they move through. Each new piece of data builds their skills, awareness, and yes, *perspective*.

USING SCHEMA PLAY THEORY TO ADVOCATE FOR FREE PLAY

The goal of this book is not only to introduce readers to the theory of play schemas, but also to discuss the ways that an understanding of the theory can help play advocates articulate the value of free play. Chapter 2 examines the benefits of play for young children, the risks of play deprivation, and barriers to free play pedagogy in early childhood settings. Chapters 3–10 will discuss each of the schemas introduced above in greater depth, discussing the value of each experience to doubts held by potential skeptics in an effort to overcome those risks and barriers.

My work with schema play theory centers on the idea that if free play advocates hope to create change and to expand access to free play in early childhood, we have to understand how to specifically connect with the audience we want to persuade and to tailor our message to their priorities. When I speak on this idea at conferences, I use a framework of "crowds" to organize these target audiences.

Persuading the Neuroscience Crowd

In this group we have folx who are very excited about the many ways we are now able to demonstrate the importance of the early years for brain growth and development because it validates our work with children birth to age 5. We know that between birth and the age of 5, more brain growth is happening than at any other time of life. Neural connections are being built at a faster rate than at any other time of life, and are strengthened or pruned based on the child's experiences and relationships. *So see, we're real professionals! We work with children during their most important brain development years!* But uh-oh . . . did this evidence change the way we plan for children and manage classrooms and expectations? Not as much as it should have! In fact, using the language of brain development without a deeper look into the ways the brain develops in these years often contributes to or supports existing elements of the academic pushdown. The discussion of the benefits of free play in Chapter 2 will explore this phenomenon further.

Persuading the SEL Crowd

SEL, or "social–emotional learning," has two buzzword claims to fame. First, SEL can be used euphemistically to discuss challenging behavior instead of being recognized as a valid and complex element of human development. SEL is commodified as a behavior management tool, a remedy to the inconvenience teachers experience when children are not easy to understand. Its second claim to fame is as part of a moral panic from groups who fear and resist human diversity. SEL includes identity development, including racial and gender identity, and so social–emotional learning is seen by some as "woke indoctrination." As I elaborate in later chapters when discussing play scenarios, there is a deeper way of thinking about what social and emotional *development* really is, how important it is to all children, and how it is supported in play. The assumption that SEL is only useful for managing behavior or indoctrinating children with woke ideologies limits our understanding of and our support for children's emotional and social lives, which thrive on play experiences. The stories in this book will show you how much more complex this area of development is.

Persuading the Parent Crowd

I got to know this crowd very, very well in my time as a child care center director. It seemed like every day I would get at least one phone call from a parent/guardian asking, "So do children *learn* things or do they just *play*?" I still have a visceral reaction to that question. Thank goodness that Katrina Macasaet and I crossed paths through her work with Zero to Three several years ago. As senior PD manager for professional innovation, she offered me an alternate perspective—these parents are advocating for their child's educational success *with the information they have been given*. With so much marketing, so many parent groups, and yes, so many early childhood programs, telling them that every experience must be "educational," and the way "educational" is defined is early academics, of course they will see play as less of a priority. I am convinced that families are the key to changing this discourse. I dream of the day that a mom calls a child care center and asks, "Do children get to play there, or are they forced to do school-like things too early?"

Schema play theory is a great tool to help shift their thinking. They know their children better than anyone, and when we name what looks random as exploration of a play schema, they see more of and become more curious about the play. One of my favorite play-advocacy moments in the last several years was a coworker texting me a photo of her toddler's plastic hot dog toy sitting on the toilet lid, and asking me, "Is this a schema?" It absolutely could be! It might be a transporting schema, a transforming schema, or a positioning and ordering schema!

Persuading the "Playing Teacher" Crowd

It is difficult to "sell" a free play pedagogy, or even a defense of more play in early childhood settings, to practitioners who wonder, "If they 'just play' all day, how am I a teacher? What do I do with my expertise and skill? How does learning happen if I'm not in charge?" In this crowd, we see people working with children from birth to age 5 in ways that look like elementary school—the teacher leading everything and making every decision, the whole group of children moving through the day as a unit, and with any nonconformity seen as a loss of teacher control.

These teachers worry that free play would encourage more misbehavior and make it impossible to ensure that goals and standards are addressed systematically. They often talk about how much they loved playing teacher as a child and have taken that memory as a sign they were *called to teach* (to which I ask, what if you just really loved dramatic play and that was a familiar context for you to reenact?). Is this too harsh? When I consider how this mentality and practice contributes to play deprivation, I don't think so.

In 1999, Jacobs and Eskridge wrote that even after receiving training in developmentally appropriate practice, adults regularly use their school memories in their work with children instead of that training. My decades of experience working with a variety of practitioners in diverse settings has shown me this is true. If I want to advocate for more play in these programs, I need to make the case that you can still be an expert, a professional, *and a "real" teacher* if children play!

Persuading the STEM Crowd

The STEM crowd is closely related to the "Playing Teacher" crowd in its focus on attempting to assign tangible academic value to young children's experiences. It's right there in the name—science, technology, engineering, math. The group believes that adults have to be in charge of the experience, with their learning standards in hand, if they are going to support this kind of learning.

You might be surprised. Every foundational skill for what is labeled STEM is deeply practiced and supported when children play. The discussion of play scenarios throughout the rest of this book will highlight how free play pedagogy *is* STEM teaching.

Each chapter of this book will include information that can be used to tailor advocacy messages to the priorities of each of these "crowds" as I identify the value of the experience described for the child's social, emotional, math, science, literacy, and brain development.

IT'S NOT ALL IN OUR HEADS

Before we continue, it is important to note that the majority of work on schema play, including Athey's original work, focuses on cognitive benefits of play experiences. I worry that this may also contribute to a focus on how play can be used to teach early academics, increasing, or at least maintaining the prevalence of a separation of the brain from the body that is rampant in early care and education discourse. It might be said that we have a schema about "learning" that is thrown into disequilibrium when we are presented with the reality that *all* learning and growth is interrelated in early childhood, and that schema play theory has many more relevant applications than just cognitive skill.

CHAPTER 2

Free Play Pedagogy
Benefits and Barriers

Free play is disappearing from young children's lives (Gray, 2011), resulting in increased issues around sensory processing, mental health, and even academic success for many children. Early care and education practitioners who acknowledge the research supporting the value of free play, and who believe play is a human right (International Play Association-USA, n.d.), have a responsibility to advocate for the return of free play to the children in our child care centers, family child care homes, preschools, and other early childhood care and education settings.

Presenting schema play theory as a tool for this advocacy requires that we examine the disconnect that exists in the field between what we *say* about the value of play and what we actually *offer* children in our settings. It is not uncommon to hear a practitioner describe themself as "play-based" when their classroom, daily schedule, and expectations of children clearly reflect a belief in adult-led, structured experiences for children. The rejection of true free play implies an adult distrust of children as competent human beings, able to guide their own learning. There is a tendency to use play-like language to manage this disequilibrium and to maintain the focus on adult priorities. (For example, phrases like "playful learning," "guided play," "play-based learning," or "scaffolded play" *sound* like play, but are still guided by adult planning and focused on adult priorities.) This disconnect is also present in conversations with families, who might want to embrace play and yet feel forced to look for more school-ish programming and environments when selecting an early childhood setting for their child.

It can be a struggle to find effective ways to interpret the language of childhood play effectively to those who are most comfortable viewing early childhood education with their adult lens of learning standards, assumptions about development, and the pressure of school readiness. The theory of schemas in children's play offers a new option for making this learning visible and for helping families and practitioners better understand how children construct knowledge through play, and to become more comfortable advocating for free play.

The American Academy of Pediatrics's position paper recognized the harmful effects of this disconnect and defends play, recommending that pediatricians prescribe play at well check-ups for young children (Yogman et al., 2018). The paper acknowledged that it is often difficult for outsiders to see the value of activities that are voluntary, fun, and without immediately obvious goals.

Their perspective provides support for using schema play theory to create change when used to connect play to the kind of learning that is easier for adults to recognize, value, and accept. As children repeatedly transport, transform, connect, position, and explore other schema, they are able to build on previous experiences, experiment with new ideas, and make relevant connections to information. This *is* learning. Chapters 3–10 of this book will examine each of the eight schemas in more depth and will offer specific guidance for understanding the play schema and using it to fight against the extinction of play in early childhood.

BENEFITS OF FREE PLAY PEDAGOGY IN EARLY CHILDHOOD

In her powerful 2017 book, *The Importance of Being Little: What Young Children Really Need From Grown Ups,* early childhood educator and school consultant Erika Christakis wrote, "Play is the fundamental building block of human cognition, emotional health, and social behavior" (p. 146). If we continue to allow play to disappear from early childhood settings, we rob children of significant opportunities to grow, develop, and learn. This section explores some of the numerous benefits of free play and its impact on children to prepare for further discussion of schema play theory and its potential efficacy as an advocacy tool.

Social and Emotional Opportunities

Improve your students' academic performances. Control the bullying problem. Build student character. Improve student attitudes. Ensure better behavior. These are some of the promises found with a basic internet search on SEL (social–emotional learning).

There is no shortage of programs or educational support products aimed at delivering social–emotional learning with the idea that SEL is something we do *to* children to better control our classrooms. The idea of SEL has become a commodity that can be sold to those hoping to change the classroom dilemma of *inconvenient children* who are seen as a distraction. They situate the teacher and the children whose behavioral compliance is interpreted as being "ready and waiting to learn" as victims. Desperate and tired adults looking for a quick solution often turn to prescribed SEL products for relief.

Rather than framing social–emotional *teaching* as something done *to* children (the frequent focus of the products and programs described above), free play pedagogy works to support healthy social and emotional *development*. It is problematic to view SEL as an after-the-problem remedy that lives outside of us. We should be looking for ways that authentic, everyday social and emotional development can be honored, practiced, and supported through play. Here are some examples of what this might look like in an early childhood setting with a free play pedagogy:

- **Self-regulation:** As Jieun is using glue in the art area, she squeezes too much out at once. Instead of sticking to the paper in the way she had planned, her collage pieces swim and are soaked in glue. She selects another piece of paper, this time squeezing the glue more lightly. She is learning that she can regulate her body in a way that is more likely to achieve her goals.
- **Social knowledge/understanding:** The teacher has added hand-held umbrellas as loose parts this week, and Kim, Luke, Elias, and Jack are at the top of the slide, with an open umbrella, trying to figure out how to all fit behind the open umbrella to go down the slide together. As they position themselves and the umbrella, they have to be aware of each other's bodies and ideas and communicate with each other.
- **Social skills:** Ann and Max have taped toilet paper tubes together to make "lookers" (binoculars) to pretend to go bird watching. They walk together through the classroom, looking through the tubes and talking about the color and size of the birds they pretend to see. After a while, Marianne (who has been watching them for a few minutes) moves closer and begins to follow them, laughing about the funny colors of birds she hears them describe. Max notices Marianne and says, "Come play with us." Ann asks the teacher to make Marianne her own set of binoculars so that she can join their game.
- **Developing a positive self-identity:** Eva found a basket of plastic apples. She takes them to the top of the indoor climber, pretends to take a bite, and then "faints" and slides down the slide with her eyes closed, pretending to be dead from the poisoned apple. Max and Caleb hurry to the top of the climber and imitate what they saw Eva doing. The game continues for several minutes. When the others imitated her play, and they

all laughed together as they played, Eva experienced herself as someone who has good ideas, who can influence others, and who is worth paying attention to.

- **Feeling empathy:** Whenever it rains, the spongy playground surface is suddenly covered in worms. Tyrese, Finn, Effy, and Gabriela worry that the worms will be "smooshed" by the other children as they run around the playground. Effy runs to the shed and brings out several buckets and they work together to save the worms. As they work together, they talk about how it would hurt the worms to be stepped on.

- **Developing feelings of competency:** Four-year-old Caleb is very interested in writing and how people's names are spelled. He is often in the writing area, using marker boards, sentence strips, and a variety of writing implements. Autumn is interested in pretend play in the dramatic play area and spends a lot of time assigning pretend roles to other players, interpreting the needs of the baby dolls, and taking on the role of parent. Jack spends most of each morning filling the toy dump truck with a variety of materials from the manipulative and math areas and driving them across the room, dumping them, and coming back for more. When they are each allowed to follow their interests and practice their ideas, their sense of competence is strengthened in a way that would not necessarily happen if they were all expected to do the same activities.

- **Recognizing and labeling emotions:** Evan and Beth are engaging in rough-and-tumble play—chasing each other and then hugging until they fall over together. After several minutes, the teacher says, "Beth, I'm looking at Evan's face and he's not smiling anymore. I wonder if he's still having fun with this game?" Over time, Beth learns to read facial cues and to wonder about others' feelings.

- **Developing a sense of community:** Five 2-year-olds stand around a water table, full of soapy water, baby dolls, washcloths, and measuring cups. They splash, hold up their bubbly hands to show each other, take turns, and pass each other the measuring cups, splash each other a little, and laugh a lot. They experience the joy of being in a community with shared interests and goals while "caring for" the baby dolls.

- **Building relationships:** Mr. Chad notices that Max and Caleb are pretending that the dramatic play kitchen is a coffee drive-through. He brings his empty coffee cup to them and asks how much it costs to get a coffee refill. The boys tell him he can't come into the coffee shop, he has to go to the drive-thru (the other side of the wooden sink structure) to get more coffee. The boys start to talk about the headsets they see "drive-through coffee people" wear. Later in the day, when they wake up from nap, Mr. Chad shows them the headsets he has made them using headbands and pipe cleaners. The coffee shop play continues. The next day, Mr. Chad brings in paper bags and coffee cups with lids from his local coffee shop to add to the play. This playful, child-led serve and return strengthens the relationship between the boys and Mr. Chad.

- **Engaging in cooperative play:** Every day for 2 weeks, the 5-year-olds in the mixed-age preschool class spend the full morning free play time "putting on a show." They talk to each other about their ideas of what the show will be and ideas change with new input from each other. They talk about what they will need for their show: chairs, tickets, a sign, an audience, and for some reason, lots of cut string taped to tables. They volunteer or assign each other to various tasks and approach other children to tell them about their show and how they are preparing.

- **Engaging in conflict resolution:** The slide on the playground is wide enough for two children to go down at once. Ethan and Mai are enjoying running up the steps, racing to the top of the slide, and then sliding down the slide together. After a few repeats of this pattern, Juanita and Denis begin to climb up the slide from the bottom as Ethan and Mai sit down at the top of the slide. Mai starts to slowly slide down, and then stops herself by holding on tightly to the sides of the slide as Denis gets near her on his way up. Juanita stands at the bottom of the slide, on the side Ethan is trying to come down. Ethan says, "Hey guys, we're tryin' to come down!" Mai says to Denis, "Walk around me." Denis and Mai maneuver around each other, and Mai continues down the slide as Denis walks up the slide behind her. Juanita moves to the other side of the slide, clear now that Denis and Mai have finished, and Ethan has a clear route to go down on his side of the slide.

Brain Development

In the 1990s, there was an explosion of awareness regarding brain research and brain development in young children, particularly from birth to age 3. This was due in large part to celebrity parent Rob Reiner's 1997 creation of the I Am Your Child Foundation and its national public awareness campaign (Jacobson, 2018). Brain development products, books, and news segments targeting parents became pervasive. In the early care and education world, this meant new opportunities for funding and for the profession to claim the elusive professional respect we had been chasing. After all, if early childhood practitioners could say definitively that the work that had been dismissed as *just day care* or *just babysitting—*or even *just playing—*could now be presented as being as important, or maybe *more* important, than that of teachers of older children, surely, we would receive that respect.

But we made a mistake. Too many early childhood folx, parents, and policymakers accepted the sound bites as data. Messaging about the research regarding brain development in early childhood seemed to be indicating that a child's brain was "emptiest" during this time period, and therefore the readiest it would ever be to have academic content poured in. Funders and policymakers interpreted this new information as a mandate for earlier ABCs and 123s. The early care and education field did not rise up and say, "Wait! That's not how this works!"

Instead of responding to the new information by wondering "What does that mean in practice?" or "How does that development happen, specifically?" many reacted with "Yes! We knew it! Earlier *is* better! Pushed down academic school-like expectations for everyone!"

So how *does* it work? Play is key!

Brain growth and development are complex, and the myths are often easier to implement in early care and education settings. After all, if the brain is the most receptive to new information at this time of life, and if brain development is presented as a "now or never" situation, it seems to make sense that what we need to do is start treating children under age 5 like school students. It's easiest to fill that empty brain with content if we provide early care and education in settings where the children sit and receive and the adults present information that is easy to recognize as being school-ish. This is a focus on teaching. I think that understanding what science tells us about brain development demands that we think instead of *how* children learn, and *children learn best by playing.*

It would be impossible to include, in one section of one chapter, every single important element of brain development. Instead, we can start with a very basic concept of this development: neural connections. Neurons are nerve cells in the young child's brain. Mine Conkbayir, in her 2017 book *Early Childhood and Neuroscience: Theory, Research, and Implications for Practice,* calls neurons the "building blocks of the brain." She describes three parts of a neuron: the cell body, dendrites, and axons. Dendrites bring information to the cell body. The axons take information away from the cell body to form connections with other neurons. These neural pathways send signals from one part of the brain to another. These pathways become key to how a child thinks and learns.

Gill Connell and Cheryl McCarthy, authors of *A Moving Child Is a Learning Child: How the Body Teaches the Brain to Think (Birth to Age 7)* (2013), explain that these neural pathways are built by early physical and sensory experiences. Another key process in this piece of brain development is myelination. Myelin is an insulating layer that forms around the axon. Myelination allows more rapid transmission of information along the neural pathways.

In 2017, the LEGO Foundation issued a white paper written by Liu and colleagues identifying five elements of play that create ideal conditions for brain development and learning in early childhood:

1. **Play is joyful.** This sparks the brain's reward centers and leads to a release of dopamine. Dopamine is key for the development of memory, attention, creativity, mental flexibility, and motivation. When a child experiences this joy, they want to stay engaged and repeat experiences. The learning is deepened because of this positive emotional experience.

2. **Play is meaningful to the child.** Deep, authentic learning happens not when a child is drilled into rote memorization, but when they can link new experiences to familiar experiences. The human brain at any age remembers information better in context. It is difficult for adults working with a group of young children to know what kind of context each individual child has. Allowing free play within a developmentally responsive environment enables children to identify their own contexts and to add new relevant information to that context by choosing and directing their own play.

3. **Play is actively engaging.** Not only does a free play pedagogy allow children to take charge of their own learning, it allows for more authentic, meaningful movement than more adult-directed, sedentary early learning practices. Movement is key to brain development. As Connell & McCarthy (2013) write, "A young child is a literal, physical creature who needs to experience life in her own way, in her own time, on her own terms and with her own body" (p. 9). An actively engaged child is also more likely to have many different experiences, each engaging a range of the child's senses. The more sensory experiences provided by active engagement, the more deeply input and information from these experiences are planted within the brain.

4. **Play is iterative.** It allows for the repetition of actions, processes, and experiences. Neural pathways require repetition to remain permanent. The more often the brain repeats an action or process, the more deeply any information from that action or process is implanted. The child who is engaged in repetition during play gains the context that makes play meaningful.

5. **Play can be socially interactive.** When children engage in social play, they have opportunities to both be and benefit from what Lev Vygotsky referred to as the "more knowledgeable other," according to his sociocultural theory (Featherstone, 2017, p. 280). They can also gain experience with healthy relationships and experience greater mental well-being. Relationships are key not just for learning, but for the emotional safety that contributes to a child's overall health and supports a child in their explorations of the world.

Free play in an environment where children experience relational safety, developmentally responsive expectations regarding the need for movement, plentiful opportunities for sensory experiences, opportunities for choice and agency, and acceptance of the child's need for repetition support the kind of brain development that is key during the first five years. These settings are far more beneficial to the growing brain than specific academic measures that marginalize free play.

School Readiness

In the United States, there is significant cultural and political pressure for intense focus on the idea of "school readiness," and the resulting obsession has taken over our practices with and expectations for young children (Farran, 2022). The focus on offering pre-K to prepare children for kindergarten (and beyond) has been pushed all the way down into infancy. Sometimes we see this as a direct, explicit expectation such as the parents who asked one of my colleagues if they offered any "gifted" programs for their 9-month-old, whom they wanted to start on a track for an Ivy League college.

At other times, the pressure can be more indirect. For example, when early childhood practitioners think, "Well, she's almost a year old, it's time to take her bottle away and train her to sleep on a cot rather than in her crib so she's ready to be a toddler," rather than, "I see where this baby is in her childhood journey, and I will trust her teacher in the toddler room to meet her there." The constant striving to get to what is next earlier, for the convenience of the adults in the next room or program, may seem ridiculous as described in this scenario, but it is accepted as a guiding strategy for many adults working with children under 5 years of age when considering school readiness. This lack of trust in, respect for, and valuing of *the child in the present* hinders growth, development, and authentic learning. It devalues play and leads to inappropriate practices in the name of "getting children ready."

While stories such as the infant teacher training the infant to be ready for toddler expectations is not explicitly framed as school readiness, it should be seen as a symptom of the ways the school readiness narrative has infected our thinking about children's learning. This focus on preparing for the future by trying to accelerate development and learning creates pressure to implement programming that is primarily concentrated on easily measured, discrete skills rather than whole child development. It leads practitioners, policymakers, and parents to expect early childhood programs to look like their familiar image of learning; academic pressure is pushed down into early childhood (Keskin, 2018). In this vision, learning only happens when an adult is in charge, when lesson plans are preplanned and administered to groups of children, when there are alphabets and shape/color/number posters hanging on the walls, and when children are passive receivers of knowledge. The learning that *is* valued often centers around reading and math skills to the exclusion of other areas of children's development.

It is also important to consider the disconnect that exists between what families, ECCE practitioners, and policymakers recognize as school readiness (counting, letter recognition, early reading, shape and color recognition, and compliance behaviors like sitting still in groups or staying in line) and most formal attempts to define school readiness. In 2018, the Regional Education Lab Northwest (Pierson, 2018) compiled a spreadsheet of state-by-state definitions of kindergarten readiness. Their research showed that only 26 states had adopted official definitions of readiness, and of those 26 definitions there are references to "early literacy" and "communication" skills (but not "reading"), and the math expectations mostly refer to "mathematical thinking." While three mention "academic" skills, 12 refer instead to "cognitive" or "intellectual" skills. There are many more skills mentioned in these definitions—like approaches to learning, social, emotional, and physical development. Words like self-regulation, attention, focus, persistence, and curiosity are also prevalent. This is a *far broader* way of thinking about school readiness than the narrow focus on letter memorization, counting, and shape and color recognition that is often the focus of early childhood programs promising "readiness."

What does this have to do with play? Play is the developmentally appropriate approach to school readiness:

- When 4-year-old George fits as many basketballs as he can into the wagon on the playground, he's raised a question about objects around him (science) and is practicing counting skills (math).
- When 20-month-old Austin gathers plastic animals and insects of various sizes and tries to fit each one into a plastic cup, he's getting experience with comparing and ordering, shape, spatial reasoning and, if uninterrupted by teacher questions or suggestions, engaging for a long period of time with materials around him (math, approaches to learning).
- When 2-year-old Alejandro balances a 1-cup measuring cup on the corner of the sand table, and uses a ½-cup measuring cup to fill it with sand, he is engaging with ideas (approaches to learning), thinking about more/less and full/empty (mathematical thinking), and getting to practice using his shoulder, elbow, wrist, and fingers (prewriting).
- When 3-year-old Abbigail puts the baby doll in the high chair and begins to pretend to feed him, she is using symbolic thinking (prereading, math), taking someone else's perspective by thinking about what a "mom" does (social skills), and using expressive language.
- When 3-year-old Kischa chooses a favorite book and snuggles up to her teacher to hear a story she has heard many times before, she begins to associate reading with a warm relationship, a pleasurable experience, and gains experience with comprehension (literacy).
- When 3-year-old Noor lines up a pool noodle from the top of the climber to the small trampoline, and tries to send a car down the tube, she is experimenting with height, angles, and size (math). She uses her gross motor (health and well-being, regulation) and fine motor skills (prewriting). She hypothesizes and makes predictions (science).
- When 5-year-olds Max, Caleb, Gabe, and Lila swing together in the large saucer swing, chanting "Eat Miss Heather!" over and over and laughing together, they are experiencing the pleasure of social relationships, showing cognitive development in their use of humor, and engaging in a cooperative project, taking and trying each other's ideas (social, emotional, intellectual skills).
- When the teacher stoops to see what has a group of children crouched close to the ground with their heads together, she

notices that they are all watching a grasshopper (science). The teacher talks to them about it, and listens to them talk about it—modeling the give and take of conversation and introducing new vocabulary (literacy).

BARRIERS TO FREE PLAY PEDAGOGY IN EARLY CHILDHOOD

The benefits and impacts discussed in the previous section provide abundant support for adopting a free play pedagogy in which adults use free play and children's choice as the main organizational idea in their planning for young children. So why is it so rare? I have identified five distinct barriers to this type of pedagogy, all of which contribute to the extinction of play in early childhood.

Barrier 1: Defining Play

In his 2009 book *Play: How It Shapes the Brain, Opens the Imagination, and Invigorates the Soul*, Stuart Brown writes that "defining play has always seemed to me like explaining a joke—analyzing it takes the joy out of it" (p. 16). However true this may be, a lack of consensus regarding what "play" actually means in our conversations about early care and education presents an obstacle to protecting play. Early childhood practitioners may have conversations about play, but one may be defining play as freely chosen exploration while the other may be defining play as adult-led activity using toys. These two people are talking about play, but they are not having the same conversation. Like good research, effective communication requires an agreed upon definition of terms.

Several years ago, a coteacher and I were talking with a child's father about the philosophy of our program. This colleague and I had not worked together for very long, but we had agreed that we wanted the program to be "play-based." When this father asked how we taught the children in our program, I replied, "You are going to see a lot of play!" My coteacher immediately added, "But it will be *play with a purpose.*" Despite our previous conversations about wanting a play pedagogy, we had not been using the same definition. I was talking about play that is voluntary, intrinsically motivated, and chosen by the child. She was talking about activities that are planned by the adult, assigned to children, and guided by adult goals, but are presented in a playful manner that uses play materials rather than worksheets. These were two strikingly different approaches to early childhood pedagogy, despite having been described using the same word.

What is implied in our various attempts to define play is distrust of the process, and by extension a distrust of children. Modifiers like *play with a purpose, purposeful play, guided play,* or *scaffolded play* reduce play to something that is meaningless unless adults are in control. After all, *play for the sake of play* couldn't possibly be what researchers and theorists present as the ideal condition for young children's learning and development, right? Surely, there *must* be something that adults need to control to make it valuable and meaningful.

As long as these arguments about the definition of play exist, feeding the uncertainty of the adult role and reinforcing our implicit distrust of children as competent learners, they will present a barrier to protecting and advocating for truly playful childhoods. Our conversations and efforts for children are going to be different based on our varied definitions. Using toys for adult-led lesson plans may be a more playful way of teaching young children than using worksheets or screens, but this practice does not provide for the free play that research supports as the best avenue for development across all domains in early childhood, and therefore it contributes to its extinction.

The variety in the language around play can also work against efforts to advocate for children's right to play. The goal of advocacy is to take a stand for a topic and try to influence others to adopt that stance. We want to express our full support for a child's right to play, for the value play brings to children's health, development, and learning. We want people to trust play. The addition of modifiers like "scaffolded play" or "purposeful play" send a conflicting message that play is not enough, that children are not competent, and that the adults who adopt a free play pedagogy are not truly teachers. This modification of our message works against our goal of ensuring playful childhoods for every child, even those attending early childhood programs.

It is therefore necessary to establish a definition to guide this book's discussion of barriers to play and the use of schema play theory as a tool for provision and advocacy. A review of play scholarship presents a clear case that it is more effective to describe aspects of an activity that would be identified as playful. Stuart Brown (2009) asserts that play is distinguishable from other activities if it is done for its own sake and not for survival, is voluntary, is fun, affects the participant's awareness of the passage of time, allows the participant to be fully in the moment, provides flexibility for the way things are seen or experienced, and causes a desire to continue or repeat the activity. Hirsh-Pasek et al. (2009) have characterized play as having no extrinsic goals and having a private reality for the player that may not be obvious to those who are not involved. Yogman et al. (2018) suggest that play involves active engagement and results in joyful discovery.

These descriptions of play provide the lens through which play will be viewed and discussed in this book.

Barrier 2: Practitioner Preparation

Personal experience and anecdotal data shared with me by interview participants and colleagues indicate that for many early care and education practitioners, college coursework related to early childhood education does not provide adequate focus on the concept of play. My formal practitioner preparation occurred in three familiar stages: an associate's degree, a bachelor's degree, and a master's degree. While many textbooks included sections on play and my graduate degree included a course specifically devoted to play, the overwhelming (and misleading) message in all three stages was that the *real* learning—the *real* teaching—happened during adult-led, didactic activities that focused strictly on the cognitive and linguistic domains, preferably easily observed and measured aspects such as letters, numbers, shapes, and colors. The textbook might say that play was an "important element of children's learning," but the practicums and assignments focused on that mythical "learning time" we seem to believe exists from 9–11 a.m. when adults pour their lesson plans into the children's empty vessels. This experience informs my practice as an early childhood education professor, and I am very intentional that every course I teach includes instruction about and experience with free play as the framework for teaching efforts, classroom design, and children's experiences. This book would be a valuable textbook for early childhood education courses to encourage educators to value free play.

Mine is not an isolated experience. In preparation for writing this book, I interviewed several people who teach college students and early educators who had participated in college courses in preparation for their work with young children. Overwhelmingly, they reported a lack of focus on play as an acceptable and effective pedagogical philosophy. One early childhood education professor reported that inclusion of play in lectures, assignments, and course reading was discouraged because play was not prioritized in the National Association for the Education of Young Children's Professional Standards and Competencies for Early Childhood Educators (NAEYC National Governing Board, 2019), which was a guide for their degree programs. She felt the standards did not explicitly include knowledge of play or implementation of play practices as necessary for early educators. Another professor reported that she did not consider play a valuable use of student time, since early childhood programs in her area were so focused on early academics and school readiness.

Degreed early childhood practitioners described coursework and experience that echoed the lack of respect for play described by the college instructors I interviewed. Many of them described a familiar disconnect—play may have been briefly touched upon, but the overwhelming message of their degree programs was that valuable learning only happened in structured activities, planned and led by adults for groups of children, with standardized goals for each activity. While there may have been discussion of the importance of freedom for children, and long periods of time for children to play, assignments and field experience focused heavily on contradictory adult-led, highly structured environments, schedules, and activities.

After hearing several of the interviewees mention the limited way play was discussed in their textbooks, I reviewed the textbooks that had been historically used in my program and found that none included more than a page here and there about play.

Adding to the question of how free play is or is not included or valued in practitioner preparation curriculum is the consideration of whether college coursework is enough to prepare and encourage people to embrace play in early childhood settings. In a 2011 study conducted by Wen et al. titled "Early Childhood Teachers' Curriculum Beliefs: Are They Consistent With Observed Early Classroom Practices," the authors found empirical evidence suggesting that the assumption that teachers' curriculum beliefs (and presumably then, their daily practices) could be shaped by teacher education programs may not be true.

Barrier 3: Cultural Barriers

The third barrier contributing to the extinction of play is presented by cultural factors. A central consideration in the discussion of these factors is the shift in educational priorities for young children since the implementation of the No Child Left Behind Act of 2001 (Yogman et al., 2018). This legislation led to a broad rejection of play and prioritized more easily measured academic standards in reading and math. This trend, often referred to as "schoolification," has resulted in increased pressure for early childhood settings to look like schools for older children and, therefore, to apply more sedentary, top-down educational practices (Morgan, 2019). Children's early years changed.

When we consider other cultural changes, such as an increase in the number of working parents, decreases in safe spaces for children to play when not attending early childhood programs, and an increase in screen use for young children, it is easy to see why play has been endangered.

Barrier 4: Parental Expectations

The cultural shifts described in the previous section have also impacted parents' (our ECCE customers) perceptions of play and learning. Parents, who long before *becoming* parents have likely been bombarded with carefully marketed messages about the need to ensure that toys, apps, television programming, and experiences are "educational," are left to support and advocate for their children's success with a false dichotomy of play vs. learning (Kane, 2016). Play is often considered to be too frivolous and random to contribute to the kind of learning they have been taught to value. Their own memories of school, combined with this messaging, may contribute to the idea that learning only happens when planned by adults.

An informal survey of family child care providers, child care center directors, and early childhood classroom teachers reported the following examples of the types of early learning experiences parents have requested for their children *under 5 years old*:

- At least a half an hour of pencil holding and name writing instruction each day for their 3-year-old
- Daily tablet time for their 4-year-old
- Letter recognition, addition, and subtraction flash cards for their 2-year-old
- Art tutoring aimed at increasing their 5-year-old's chances of acceptance into a private elementary school
- Worksheets and homework folders to ensure that their 5-year-old would "stay ahead" of her peers

These cases exemplify the ways in which well-meaning parents are looking *past* play toward priorities that seem more sufficiently school-like and competitive. The most common requests from parents reported in these interviews centered around early name writing, handwriting, letter recognition, sight words, numerical skills, and a general idea of "structure." When these are the presumed measures of real learning, it is easy to see how long periods of free play would seem like a waste of children's time and parents' money. When asked "Why can't you just offer more play in your program?," the practitioner's answer is, too often, "Parents ask for academics." For parents who equate learning with strictly academic literacy and math skills, play is a hard sell.

Barrier 5: Practitioner Attitudes

A lack of coursework and field experience regarding free play, combined with the parental pressures practitioners often face, places the onus of ensuring that free play is accessible in early childhood settings on those in the field. Practitioners must themselves hold a strong belief in the value and efficacy of play in children's early learning. Unfortunately, there are indications that the attitudes of these practitioners regarding free play present another barrier. Even for practitioners who claim to believe that children learn best through play, they still struggle to implement that belief, resulting in a lack of support for play (Lemay et al., 2016). Cultural and parental pressures have led to academic programming from practitioners that replaces or limits play (Kane, 2016) in the name of "school readiness" (Brierley, 2018). Academic programming and structured, adult-led, school-like activities are easier responses to pressure for academic achievement (Howard, 2010). A focus on limited academic outcomes stems from a view of children as deficient (Brierley, 2018) often shared by parents and teachers. For teachers who are not confident in their play practice, it is easier to reject child-initiated play for adult-controlled practice (Howard, 2010).

Each of the following chapters offers a deep investigation into schema play theory and its usefulness as a framework for advocating to skeptics and naysayers, or even to those who embrace free play theoretically, but are unsure how to make it work in the "real world" of their early childhood classroom. I will share stories of real-life schema play, gathered during years of observing and wondering about children's ideas and choices. For each story, I write about the value of the experience for the child's social–emotional development, school readiness, and brain development as if I were talking to those "crowds" I wrote about in Chapter 1. Using schema play—the thing we notice the child doing—as the starting point, I walk you through the ways we can craft advocacy and education efforts to specific audiences and stakeholders.

CHAPTER 3

The Transforming Schema

- Three-year-old Nadia breaks an icicle off of the shade over the slide and uses it to "write" in the snow that has covered the playground.
- A group of 3-, 4- and 5-year-olds place plastic orange cones from the obstacle course in the center of their camping pretend play and call it the "campfire."
- Four-year-old Marianne puts her stuffed toy "Bear Bear" into the high chair in dramatic play and calls herself "Mommy" as she pretends to prepare his lunch.
- In the block area, 3-year-old Jin repeatedly stacks several blocks, knocks them down, and stacks them again.

These children are all exploring a *transforming* schema.

WHAT IS A TRANSFORMING SCHEMA?

In a transforming schema, children change materials or themselves from one thing into another. They mix up materials like paint or playdough. They invent different ways to use materials, their bodies, or their voices. Transforming explorations may sometimes look like "misbehavior"—knocking down block towers or using loud voices. A schematic lens can help us to look beyond our traditional responses to these kinds of actions and see them as valuable experiences and not as disruptions.

TRANSPORTING STORY: ANN AND MIGUEL

The large plastic bowls from yesterday's playdough-making activity are drying on the countertop next to the children's handwashing sink. Ann (5 years old) picks up the largest bowl and starts to talk to 4-year-old Miguel, recalling the mixing they had done together the day before. She says, "Let's mix new stuff!" and they each take a bowl to the table in the science area. Miguel goes to the water table and brings back two measuring cups, which they both use to bring water from the sink to their bowl.

Ann turns to the science shelf and finds cotton balls, straws, and popsicle sticks. She and Miguel both add these items to their water and stir. Ann says, "Ew, the cotton is gooey now." Miguel says, "Tear it like this!" and shows her how he breaks his cotton balls into smaller pieces before he adds them to the water.

Miguel asks me if he can put some paint in his mixture. I nod and he goes to the art area and carries a gallon jug of red paint back, using the pump nozzle to add several squirts to his mixture. Ann watches as his water and the cotton balls change colors. She walks to the art area and comes back with markers. She takes the lid off the blue marker and dips it into the water. She sees a small amount of blue spread into the water. She says, "I want a lot more of blue in my mix." She drops the whole marker into the water. Together, they watch the blue spread from the marker out into the water. Miguel walks over to Gia, who is playing on the other side of the room, and says, "We did red and blue in our mixes!"

Ann's and Miguel's Social Experience

Ann and Miguel bring very different social skills and experiences to this play exploration. Ann is very comfortable interacting with other children, directing group play, and sharing ideas. While these are all skills listed as positive elements of social development, some adults have labeled her as "bossy" and have tried to stop what they see as an antisocial behavior. Miguel has a language delay that makes it more difficult for him to be in conversation with his peers or to share his ideas. He often stands outside of play, observing but not joining. This interaction between them, as they conduct their experiments, offers each of them important experiences in becoming (and being seen as) socially competent.

As they play alongside each other, Miguel following Ann's original idea but eventually adding his own suggestions, and then sharing his excitement with Gia, is an example of peers being what Lev Vygotsky called the "more knowledgeable other" (Featherstone, 2017, p. 280) As each scaffolds the other to stretch their own skills, I would suggest that peers in play are the most authentic "more knowledgeable other." They rise above having been corrected for bossiness, having been afraid to join play, and having had their previous experiences perceived as socially disruptive or deficient.

Ann's and Miguel's Emotional Experience

When children like Ann and Miguel spend hours every day, 5 days a week, with a group of same-age children, they may face stressors that would not be present in other settings. Many of these stressors come from the pushed down academic pressures that push *out* play. A teacher who feels pressured (or prefers) to treat early childhood experiences like *school* in order to meet inappropriate academic expectations may not have allowed Ann and Miguel to have the time, the choice, or the understanding for them to follow their ideas and play in this independent way. Stressful situations like this often result in a decrease of oxytocin (a hormone that impacts bonding and relationships) and dopamine (neurotransmitters that can be essential for things like executive function and motivation). Children who experience this decrease repeatedly in those days and hours spent in early childhood program may face future difficulties as adults (Conkbayir, 2017). Ann and Miguel are instead offered space and support to follow their ideas, to feel joy in their play, and to enjoy sharing ideas with each other. They do not face those stressors, and their healthy emotional development is supported.

Ann's and Miguel's School Readiness Experience

Math. It is easy for those of us who work with young children to feel most comfortable with math that primarily involves number recognition and vocabulary. Thinking and planning in terms of *arithmetic only* comes more naturally to us. However, in Ann's and Miguel's transforming play, we see the broader scope of *mathematics*, or the theoretical aspects of this area of learning. When Miguel hears Ann's cotton ball problem (submerging the whole cotton ball in the water felt "gooey" and was unpleasant), he makes a prediction that pulling the cotton ball into smaller pieces might lead to a different result. His experience of decomposing the cotton ball gave him data that Ann could use in her own investigation.

When Miguel wanted to transform his water from clear to having a color, he made a plan to try adding paint. Ann saw the transformation that occurred and wanted to replicate it. Her plan was to get her own paint from the art area, but when she saw the markers, she saw other possibilities and developed her own prediction to test. Ann compared the way dipping the marker into her water led to results that were different from Miguel's paint transformation. She wanted a more dramatic color change, like she had seen in Miguel's water. She drew the conclusion that she had not added enough color by just dipping the marker in the water. Her plan was to then add the *whole* marker. This allowed her to establish the fact that using the marker, either a little bit or a lot, still did not lead to the full color change that she was trying to achieve.

When reframed through the transforming schema play model, what looked to some of the adults like simply messy play, wasteful practice, or incorrect use of materials can be understood as deeply engaging mathematical theory in practice.

Literacy. This transforming exploration may not seem like a literacy experience, because of our tendency to assume that literacy is mostly about letter recognition and sound production and therefore must be planned and led by an adult. However, Ann's and Miguel's experience is certainly contributing to their language and literacy development and is providing vital foundational support for letter recognition and sound production.

Ann is motivated to engage in conversation with Miguel, listening to his ideas rather than just instructing him on his role in the play. Miguel is motivated to share his ideas with Ann because he feels safe in the shared play experience. In their book, *Shifting the Balance: 6 Ways to Bring the Science of Reading into a Balanced Literacy Classroom* (2021), Burkins and Yates suggest that "routines for building speaking and listening skills are easily woven across the entire learning day. These instructional strategies do not require fancy materials, specialized training, or big schedule changes. They simply require a commitment to be intentional about bringing the classroom alive with spoken language and conversation" (p. 24). Ann's and Miguel's transforming exploration reminds us that protecting free play is part of an intentional routine that invites spoken language and rich conversation not just with adults, but with their peers.

Science. In the beginning of this interaction, Ann used prior experience to raise questions about other ways to use the mixing bowls. She raised more questions about the materials on the science shelf, as is evidenced by her experiments. When she expressed her discomfort with the cotton balls, Miguel wondered how he might help her. This question led to his suggestion that she change the way she used the materials to solve her problem.

More questions were raised for Ann, when she walked to get paint and wondered instead if the markers would help her achieve her desired effect. This process of wondering, of raising questions about the ways materials can be used and altered to achieve a goal, is a necessary skill for scientific experimentation. If I had inserted myself and stopped any of these steps, telling Ann and Miguel, "That's not how you use these materials," I would have reinforced the idea that there is only one correct way to use materials and suppressed this important STEM skill.

Ann's and Miguel's Brain Development Experience

The LEGO Foundation's work on neuroscience and play includes discussion of five characteristics of playful experiences that support brain growth. One of these characteristics is "socially interactive." The scenario above exemplifies the kinds of rich social exchanges that are more prevalent in free play than in adult-guided activities. Ann and Miguel follow their own play ideas but also build on each other's ideas while having a conversation about those ideas and the results they see from their experiments. Socially interactive experiences like this are beneficial for the development of cognitive flexibility and of mental processes that will help Ann and Miguel interpret and understand the perspectives of others.

Further Discussion

I am sure that some readers cringed a bit, or were shocked, as they read this story; it may have seemed like a waste of materials or that I was not teaching the children to be respectful of materials and of the classroom. This may be a budget reaction, or it may be a value reaction. Of course, if I had limited access to markers, I would have talked with Ann, explained that if we used the markers for her experiment, we would not have markers for art. Together, Ann and I could then have come up with an alternative idea. In fact, when I saw her make this choice, I *did* suggest that we would run out of markers if she followed her plan. Ann was a leader, not easily fooled by my conditioned reaction, and responded, "I know that there are a lot of boxes of markers in the cupboard. Can I show you?'

If we approach the issue from a value perspective, then I must ask myself, "Why do I value the markers more than I value Ann's initiative?" Here is another instance where a knowledge of schema play theory helps me make an intentional decision—thinking about Ann's idea in terms of the transforming schema helps me say yes more often. As Louis et al. (2013) write, "It is the responsibility of the practitioner to ensure that schematic play is noticed, valued and given time."

Seeing children through the lens of their schema play has given me permission to move out of the traditional view of teaching young children through direct instruction, which too often focuses on fixing deficits in the children we work with. Curriculum that requires that we assess children based on linear standards is limiting. It forces us to see first what children *cannot* do. It forces us to plan adult-led, controlled activities and to adhere to schedules that focus on moving all the children in the group to meet the same standards at the same times. It forces us to measure success in terms of achieving standardization, and individual children become adversaries when they continue to "lag behind."

What a schema play lens helps me see is the competence of children, their individuality, and the ways I can support their growth and learning even if I don't control every element of the "curriculum." I would suggest that the reliance on a system where all children in a certain age range are expected to achieve adult priorities at the same time, and where success is therefore developmentally impossible, can lead to teacher burnout. I want my teaching to be *developmentally informed* (making decisions based on developmental knowledge I have accumulated over my years of working with children and studying development) and *developmentally responsive* (making decisions based on what I am learning about development from the individual children in front of me).

I have learned a lot about schema play theory, and that gives me information about the ways I can set up my environment and the materials I hold in that space based on what Chris Athey's work tells me about development through play. As I notice and wonder about the schema explorations I see, the children teach me what I need to maintain or add to my space, in this moment, to respond to their current development. Success is no longer measured by unrealistic standards for a group, but by the growth of the individuals I see and support every day. When we operate from a deficit model, and our standards are not developmentally responsive or informed, we put the child in harm's way, but we also put ourselves in harm's way when we face potential burnout or day-to-day stressors.

TRANSFORMING STORY: JERROLD

Five-year-old Jerrold attends an early childhood classroom that is designed to support preschool-age children with a variety of speech and language delays. Jerrold has been diagnosed with a developmental language delay. He is an enthusiastic storyteller and conversationalist, but he is difficult for others to understand. This impacts his peer interactions, and he often plays alone or only with the adults who can more easily understand him.

Each week, the early childhood specialist selects a focus book to read together every morning. This week's book has been *The Amazing Erik* by Mike Huber. In the story, a boy named Erik explores a water table with blue coloring added to the water. As he explores, he exclaims, "Airdah taroo!"

Jerrold's teachers have anticipated increased interest in the water table based on having read this story and want to offer opportunities that revisit some of the elements and vocabulary from the story through the water play. They have added a stand that stretches across the length of the water table and holds a variety of funnel sizes above the water. They have also left some blue liquid watercolor paint near the water table.

Jerrold often chooses sensory play and transforming opportunities like painting and inventing different ways to use materials, so the teachers have him in mind as they set up for this water play.

Jerrold began to play in the water. First, he stirred the water with his hands, making "swooshing" noises with his mouth. He scooped water with measuring cups and poured it into the funnel, trying to get his hands under the funnel in time for some water to run over them. He played in this way, pouring and "catching" for several minutes, his eyes glued to the water and to his hands. He exclaimed "Airdah taroo!" and looked expectantly at his teacher, who responded "Airdah taroo!" As Jerrold turned his head back to the water, he noticed the blue liquid watercolor, and added it to the water table, through the funnels. Initially he was interested in watching the blue stream down the funnels. He began to stir the water with his hands again. It began to turn blue, and Jerrold said, "Wow!" This caused other children to look over at what he was doing.

Two children came over to watch Jerrold at the water table. He showed them several times how his hands looked blue in the water, but not blue when he took them out of the water. As he and these two peers played in the water together and called "Airdah taroo!" back and forth, Jerrold was part of a successful, rewarding communicative exchange with peers.

Jerrold's Social Experience

Jerrold has been identified as having a developmental language disorder, a communication disorder that can impact a child's learning, understanding, and use of language. In Jerrold's case, there are issues with intelligibility—he is difficult to understand. He is very expressive, using facial expressions, gestures, and his favorite—slapstick humor—but it is difficult for adults and children to understand what he is trying to say when he speaks. At times, this limits his social interactions, which can have a negative impact on his relationships.

Children at this age learn how to be in a relationship by literally *being in relationships*. Their "developmental trajectory is critically mediated by appropriate, affective relationships with loving consistent caregivers as they relate to children through play" (Ginsburg et al., 2007, p. 183). Jerrold often engages in solitary play, and we suspect it is because of the frustration he experiences when others don't understand what he is trying to say. But as he explores the transforming schema and connects it to the words in the book we all read together, we know what he is saying. We repeat it back and connect with each other. We have fun together. We build our relationship with Jerrold.

Jerrold's Emotional Experience

Jerrold's transforming play is an opportunity for him to engage with others using his sense of humor rather than his speech. As he draws us in and we join in his laughter, he gains confidence and sees that he can have an active, positive impact on those around him. We can think of this in terms of Bronfenbrenner's bioecological systems theory. American psychologist Urie Bronfenbrenner introduced this theory in 1979, suggesting that each child was nested within four systems of influence (the microsystem, the mesosystem, the exosystem, and the macrosystem), and that the child's interaction with each system would drive their development. Jerrold's experiences here fall within the microsystem, which is the system most directly influencing his early life. His interactions with his early childhood teachers and the setting are influencing his development. Jerrold's sense of humor is a "demand characteristic," defined by Hayes et al. (2023) as "qualities of the child that can invite or discourage reactions from the social environment" (p. 20) and impact a child's development of self-identity. As Jerrold plays with the ways he can transform his hands and the water, he makes us laugh and move closer to him. Some children join in the play and imitate him as they communicate with actions and laughter.

Jerrold's School Readiness Experience

Math. In this scenario, Jerrold's teachers have used their knowledge of both schema play and their observations of Jerrold. They respect his deep interest in the sensory table and in water play. As they prepare to share the book and to use the water and blue coloring to reinforce vocabulary, they know Jerrold will be an active explorer! This proactive planning gives them an opportunity to look for ways to provide mathematical language to describe the transformations they see in his play. The play is initiated by Jerrold, supported and planned for by his teachers, and extended by waiting for him to show his thinking through his actions. The teachers can then narrate his play, incorporating mathematical language. They can describe the amount of coloring added to the water to make changes (more, less). They can talk about how much larger the children's hands look when they are under water (wider, bigger). They can call attention to how much darker the children's hands look in the dark blue water than out of the water.

Literacy. Jerrold is having fun imitating the actions and made-up language from *The Amazing Erik*, which tells me that he has an ongoing connection to the story and that he enjoyed hearing the book. He is learning that reading books can be a fun, joyful experience, and that is one of the biggest motivating factors for young children's emerging literacy. We sat together in our morning Community Time to read the book aloud, and because it tickled Jerrold's funny bone, the story stays with him throughout the day. It motivates him to incorporate other literacy experiences throughout the nonreading portions of the day and to want to hear it again. As his teacher, I can use what I notice to select future books that will engage him—he likes books that have funny words, big actions, and a story that can connect to his real life. I can use this information to reinforce his experience of reading as enjoyable.

Narrative skills are an important precursor for reading comprehension, and we see this emerging for Jerrold as he imitates Erik at the water table. When young children tell their own stories, retell stories from books, or recall activities from the day, they are learning about story structure and can begin to predict what comes next in a story and think about characters and settings. Jerrold's narrative skills are emerging. We cannot always understand his narratives from his oral language alone, but by using the words from the book and imitating the ways Erik plays with the water and color and using his actions, Jerrold tells us what he remembers from the book. Reading comprehension refers to the ability to decode the print on the pages of a book, incorporate the illustrations, and understand what is happening as they decode. Practicing retelling stories is a really meaningful way for Jerrold to begin his journey toward reading comprehension.

Science. Jerrold's transforming play reminds us that science is not just about memorizing facts or organized experiments chosen by the teacher. For young children, providing large stretches of time for children to investigate materials and follow questions they are curious about is a much more meaningful STEM priority than an adult performance of controlled activities or direct instruction of science trivia. As Jerrold follows his chosen interest, he joyfully participates in what Epstein (2014) describes as "a lively process that involves observing, predicting, experimenting, verifying and explaining" (p. 157).

Jerrold's Brain Development Experience

Once again, the LEGO Foundation's work on the neuroscience of learning through play provides information about the transforming play schema we see in this scenario. In their white paper on learning through play, Liu et al. (2017) state that neuroscience has shown that "emotions are integral to neural networks responsible for learning" (p. 4). When Jerrold experiences joy in his schema play, he experiences a higher dopamine level. Higher dopamine levels can be connected with memory, cognitive flexibility, and sustained attention.

Further Discussion

One of the primary uses of a teacher's knowledge of schema play theory is to be a guide for noticing individual children's "threads of thinking" and finding ways to support the schemas we see them exploring. The children tell us so much about themselves through their play choices and actions, which gives us opportunities every day to truly follow their lead. I think often about how this curriculum choice, which truly follows the interest we see emerging in children's play, stands in contrast to the way I typically see "emergent curriculum" being enacted in early childhood classrooms. While the typical method starts with children's interests and questions, it can in practice continue as curriculum guided by adult priorities and themes.

A few years ago, a colleague and I discussed our frustration with an article that had been published in an early childhood journal about emergent curriculum. It told a story of two pre-K teachers who had noticed increased interest in the water play table in their classroom. The teachers noticed the children's interest in the water and decided to use that interest to draw them in to an "exploration" of water conservation—a decidedly adult goal. With schema play, we can zoom in tighter to what the actual interest that we are noticing in the child really is. Was it the turning of the water wheel? Was it the temperature of the water? Was it the changes made when blue coloring was added? I only know how to meet Jerrold where he is and authentically support his interests when I look for these kinds of clues. A framework like schema play theory helps guide me to where Jerrold is.

SUPPORTING THE TRANSFORMING SCHEMA IN YOUR PLAY SPACE

- Extend your thinking about "dramatic play" beyond common adult-selected themes of housekeeping, grocery stores, and post offices and allow space for different types of power play. Playing "bad guys," superheroes, and even weapon play are ways of exploring a transforming schema and can be valuable for children's development.

- Keep a good collection of loose parts going! Loose parts (like cardboard tubes, ribbons, egg cartons, old DVDs, fabric scraps, rocks, and sticks) are the ultimate open-ended transforming prop. Asking children's families to collect and donate loose parts is also a great way to advocate for play and to offer a meaningful way for them to be involved in the early childhood program.
- Reflect on your attitudes and comfort level around messy play. What tools can you add to make cleanup easier? Collect adult-sized T-shirts for children to wear over their clothes. Conduct a "cost/benefit analysis" about mess—what benefit do children lose if we say no to messy play?
- Practice using science and math vocabulary as you narrate children's transforming play. Move away from quizzing about color and "What is that?" toward making simple occasional statements about what you see children trying in their transforming play and incorporate vocabulary like *more/less, full/empty, less than, sticky, smooth*. It helps me to have lists of this kind of vocabulary around the room to refer to.

CHAPTER 4

The Trajectory Schema

- Three 2-year-olds are running together down the hall. One stops, and the others imitate. They all start to run again, and another stops. The other imitate her. This play continues for several minutes.
- Five-year-old Michael spends most of the outdoor play time packing snowballs and throwing them at various targets—the brick wall, the slide, the sunshade covering the center of the playground.
- Three-year-old Tristan hangs from the edge of the shade at the top of the wide slide, swinging his body back and forth a few times before letting go and sliding down.
- Four-year-old Sammy draws several horizontal lines across a piece of paper, then takes another piece of paper and repeats this process.

These children are exploring the *trajectory* schema.

WHAT IS A TRAJECTORY SCHEMA?

In the trajectory schema, children explore horizontal, vertical, and diagonal movements of materials and of themselves. They make things fly through the air and move their bodies through space in different ways. There may be an interest in building and knocking down, to explore the properties of the building materials as they fall. Children may find ways to explore trajectories during art by flicking paint, splattering with tools, using squirt bottles, or tearing paper. These children show a deep curiosity about how things move.

TRAJECTORY STORY: DAVINA

It's afternoon free play time in the 3-and-4-year-old classroom in a child care center, and 3-year-old Davina's whole attention is on the gravelly sand and the play props in one of the sensory tables. She's been at the table for 20 minutes and shows no signs of leaving! For a while, Davina is the only child at the sand table. She holds a measuring cup in each hand and scoops with them both at the same time, then she pours them both into a bucket. She repeats this twice, and on the third pour, one cup gets in the way of the other. The sand from the top cup spills out over the lower cup and misses the bucket. She repeats this a few times before positioning one cup under the other and pouring from both at the same time, from different heights. She laughs out loud as the sand and gravel mix moves in a different, and less controlled, way.

Twin 3-year-old boys notice her laughing and move to the sand table to watch her. She shows them the way she's been playing with the sand and they grab measuring cups and imitate her. They laugh together. Davina puts one of the measuring cups down and begins to pour the sand over her empty hand, spreading her fingers, then moving them back together, watching as the sand slips through or stops. One of the boys says, "Watch me!" and shows Davina that he is imitating what she did. Davina repeats the action back for him. She and the boys laugh together.

After a while, Davina switches to a larger cup and begins to experiment with pouring sand from the cup to the bucket from different heights. She reaches as high as she can and pours the sand into the bucket repeatedly. She is watching the sand intently as it forms straight or arced lines from her hand to the bucket.

Davina's Social Experience

Davina began her trajectory play on her own, alone at the sand table. Her laughter caught the attention of the two boys who had been playing near her but in different ways. They were intrigued enough to leave their play and join Davina. As they watched and imitated her, they all laughed together. The boys stayed for a while and then moved back to their own play ideas.

Davina and the boys are exhibiting age-appropriate friendship skills as they connect over the trajectory play. Conversations are a key element in developing friendships, and their play is a conversation. You can see the give and take as they watch each other, laugh at each other's actions, and use language to stay connected. We see here an example of what Garry Landreth (2023) meant when he wrote, "children express themselves more fully and more directly through self-initiated spontaneous play than they do verbally because they are more comfortable with play" (p. 9). There is a verbal element of their conversation, but the real conversation happens in their native language—play.

Davina's Emotional Experience

Sand tables and other sensory opportunities are often spoken of in terms of their value in calming children. This is often an adult-centric goal—if children experience emotions that are too intense or challenging for the structure of the program day and schedule, we can refer them to the sand for relief rather than working through the emotion with the child or slowing down to allow for the emotion. Sand play *can* be effective in this way, but I see Davina's trajectory play in the sand table benefiting her in a different way. I watched her engage deeply with her ideas and her play choice. I saw the wonder she found in watching the sand move through space in different ways. She was experiencing a state of regulation she had achieved on her own, experiencing herself as the holder of powerful ideas and as an influence on others. In this way, the sand play contributes to her emotional development and to the tone of the classroom.

Davina's School Readiness Experience

Math. Early educators and parents often lament that they try to engage their preschool-age children in math "activities" but find that they don't hold the children's attention. Davina's interest in the trajectory of the sand as she experimented kept her focus on mathematics as she used the measuring cups and buckets for most of the hour of free play time that I observed. She began her play by using the standard measurement tools that had been provided and got more data about size, comparison, concepts like full and empty, distance, and speed than she would have in a teacher-led activity because she chose the context for that learning rather than being told how to use the materials, what she should be looking for, and when she was done.

Literacy. As Davina's hands move up and down or stay still so that the sand can fall over them, her eyes look at the cup as she raises it, at her hand as the sand pours over, and then back up to the hand holding the measuring cup. In all her explorations in the sand, she is building her eye-body coordination. Physical development's impact on literacy development is often systematically overlooked and devalued in early childhood as we hyper-focus on letter recognition and letter sounds. Davina's practice with her eye-body coordination is training her eyes and hands to work as a team in ways that are vital to future literacy instruction, when she will be expected to maneuver the pencil about the paper while writing (Benge, 2023).

Science. Davina's sand exploration falls into a trajectory schema as she experiments with how the sand moves as it falls through space between her hands or the measuring cups and the bucket or the sand table. She sees the difference between this motion as the sand falls from high and low and how hitting another object (her hand or the bucket) changes the direction of the falling sand. As she plays in this way, she is demonstrating scientific curiosity. She repeats actions that cause an interesting effect, like pouring sand over her hand or from as high as she can reach up, and then she continues to try new ways of watching the sand fall through space and over objects.

Davina's Brain Development Experience

This story offers a good example of the distinction between an "enrichment activity" and "play." For a child's brain to grow, we often assume that it requires an adult to be in charge with a scripted, planned activity to "enrich" the child's brain. However, research points in the opposite direction and places more importance on the kind of freely chosen, child-directed play that Davina is engaged in. This confusion can be traced to American neuroscientist Marian Diamond and her work in the 1960s. Diamond found that play was an essential contributor to brain development by studying the brain growth of rats. She found that playing with "rat toys" and socializing with other rats led to increases in brain growth and did not see similar growth in rats who merely had their surroundings changed or were offered various challenges. Later in her career, Diamond explained that "Back in the early 1960s, women had to struggle to be taken seriously as scientists. I was already seen as this silly woman who watched rats play, so I did avoid words like 'toys' and 'play'" (Brown, 2009, p. 33). She instead used the word "enrichment," which has been interpreted as a greater level of outside control than existed in her experiments. Davina is getting the kind of input that Diamond found contributed to dramatic brain development as she engages in her self-directed trajectory play.

Further Discussion

In many early childhood settings, when children are allowed to freely play, adults move away from them to complete other tasks. They may work on paperwork, clean, or just chat with each other, interacting only when children do something they want to stop. It seems that they don't value children's play, and so they assume free play time is not as valuable as other elements of the daily schedule. It's part of the deficit view that so many adults project on to children—they are not yet adults, so they are not yet good enough, and we must fix them. I think one of the most exciting things about schema play is the competence it acknowledges in the child. As Louis et al. (2013) remind us, "young children are systematic, methodical, and logical as they gather information through their senses and movement, as they interact with people, objects and the environment."

Watching Davina's trajectory play, I can put myself in both mindsets. If I had not been educated about the value of free play or was just not curious about the ways I saw her playing, her actions would seem pointless. She's just standing there scooping and pouring sand? Okay—but later I'll try and teach her something meaningful related to my goals. Schema play theory gives me a different way to see the play. It gives me a framework to exercise curiosity as I wonder what might *she* be wondering? What hypotheses might she be working out? What can I learn about her thinking as she tries the different ways of pouring and scooping and adjusts her actions? What can I appreciate about the joy she may be feeling as she plays? I can see her system, her methods, and her logic.

If I had stopped this play and tried to teach her the "right" way to play in the sand ("Keep it close to the table so it doesn't get out on the floor," or "Which scoop is bigger? What could you make?"), she would have missed out on rich experiences. I don't think there is anything I could directly teach in any of the developmental or learning areas discussed above that would give Davina or any of the other children in the group the same depth of learning and authentic foundational experience she found in her own trajectory play.

TRAJECTORY STORY: JADEN

It is a rainy day and 4-year-old Jaden's preschool teachers have decided to stay inside instead of going to the playground. They rearrange the room to allow for more active play—bringing the climbing structure out to the middle of the floor, bringing the small trampoline out of the storage room, and adding pool noodles for chasing and swordfight games.

Jaden jumps on the trampoline for a minute or so, and then moves to the climbing structure, where he can climb up the side and then go down the slide. He moves back and forth between climbing up the side and going down the slide and then climbing up the slide, over the top and down the side.

Another child has brought some cars to the slide and is rolling them down. The children laugh together as the cars spin around and then careen off the edge or side of the slide. The child who brought the cars moves on to play in another area while Jaden continues to explore the cars and the slide.

He moves the trampoline across the floor, leaving it in front of the slide, and goes back up to roll cars down. He says, "I want the car on the trampoline," but the car repeatedly misses the trampoline, falling off the side of the slide instead.

Jaden sees the pool noodles and brings one to the climbing structure—positioning it over the slide, aimed toward the trampoline, and tries to fit the car through the noodle. He sees the car is too big to fit inside the pool noodle and tries to make it fit by pushing harder. The pool noodle falls out of his hand.

The teacher who has been watching this play asks Jaden if she can try an idea. He nods and hands her the pool noodle. She cuts the pool noodle in half lengthwise, and hands one half to Jaden. Together, they work on holding the noodle and trying to run the small car down its rut to see if it can land on the trampoline. Sometimes the car falls off the noodle, and sometimes it stays on, but it always misses the trampoline. After several minutes, Jaden hands the pool noodle back to the teacher and walks away.

Jaden's Social Experience

On the surface, it might not seem that Jaden's trajectory play would have offered much opportunity to foster his social development. He interacts briefly with a peer before his solitary trajectory play begins, and then with the teacher as she stands nearby and watches the exploration unfold. His play itself is solitary, but is supported by both the peer and the teacher. The play started when the peer brought cars to the slide and they laughed and rolled the cars down the slide. As it continued, Jaden often looked to the teacher and laughed when his various hypotheses did not work out as he had predicted. This laughter is key to the social element of this schema example. In an article discussing humor and social understanding, Paine et al. (2020) write that "shared humor is a central feature of children's close relationships and a universal, integral part of human experience" (p. 592). As I write this, I think about how often I have seen adults separate children who are laughing together and scold them for being disruptive instead of recognizing the laughter as a key social experience.

Jaden's Emotional Experience

We've seen an increase in the use of the word *resilience* regarding young children since the COVID-19 pandemic, often in contexts that rely on rhetoric that children have amazing resilience and so we don't have to worry about how their stressful experiences might impact their development. But resilience does not happen automatically. Resilience can be defined as the ability to bounce back from setbacks and is a learnable set of skills, not an inborn quality automatically installed in children. In Jaden's trajectory play we see an example of this learning in action. In his efforts to find a way to move the car down the pool noodle and onto the trampoline, he safely experiences challenges, trial and error, and persistence when things are difficult. His confidence grows as he takes control of the challenge, and as he knows the teacher is there to support him if needed but trusts him to try his ideas. Repeated experiences like this will build Jaden's resilience for stressful events.

Jaden's School Readiness Experience

Math. While the teacher did not take over or interrupt Jaden's play until he indicated he needed her help, she did model mathematical language as she watched his experiment unfold. As she observed and narrated, she said things like:

- "It fell off in the middle and didn't get to the bottom!"
- "Oh well, back to the top to try again."
- "You moved the trampoline closer. You thought it might be too far away."

While he was experiencing these concepts in his repeated attempts to roll the car onto the trampoline, the teacher's deep noticing and objective narration enabled Jaden to connect his concrete experiences to more abstract concepts that will be important for later school math without trying to push adult-led formal mathematics into the play.

Literacy. In his trajectory exploration, Jaden had to hold several bits of information in his mind to remember what he had already tried, to think about the materials he knew were in his environment, and to recall what worked or didn't work before. This kind of experience builds working memory—an element of executive function that connects directly to future reading comprehension. *Comprehension* requires the ability to decode the symbols on the page, understand the meaning of the words and of the sentences the words create, and use background knowledge to make meaning of it all. Jaden's practice using working memory builds his skill in keeping information active in his mind for the short period of time he played in this way. This is also how he will manage the elements of reading comprehension listed above.

Science. Jaden invented and carried out his own research as he worked on his trajectory problem. His goal was to roll the car down the slide so that it would land on the trampoline at the bottom. He observed the fact that the car was rolling off the slide before reaching the bottom and he inferred that he needed a tool to keep the car in place all the way down the slide. His hypothesis was that he could use a pool noodle to keep the car in place and successfully land on the trampoline. His prediction was that the car would fit inside the pool noodle and roll down. His investigation led him to try to just push the car harder when it did not fit into the small opening in the pool noodle. He experimented, repeating attempts several times, making small adjustments each time. He eventually collaborated with the teacher, who asked if she could try an idea. This is a much more authentic experience with research and scientific curiosity than an adult could have preplanned for him.

Jaden's Brain Development Experience

Movement is key to early brain development, and in this play, Jaden is moving his body in big, self-directed ways. O'Connor and Daly (2016) remind us that "movement stimulates the neurological system that fires and wires the brain, forming a multitude of connections that lay important foundations for the young child's future learning" (p. 10).

One of the consequences of our obsession with early academics and whole-group participation in adult-led activities in the name of getting children *ready to learn* is an unhealthy prioritization of sitting, waiting, watching, and passively listening to a teacher. Some of this can be attributed to the misconceptions about brain development research described in Chapter 2, as we have been frightened about missing a major window for learning. The result is a narrow focus on easily planned and measured math and reading skills. The result is the loss of the authentic, child-led movement that the research really points to. In his self-directed trajectory play, Jaden got valuable experience in all the "readiness" domains while moving his body in ways that contribute to the neural connections and brain growth that is so important in the early years.

Further Discussion

A benefit of understanding schema play is that the theory can help us reframe children's actions that are otherwise confusing or challenging for us, especially those that are often seen as misbehavior. In Jaden's story, because he was allowed to play out his ideas, we can see that he intended no disrespect to any of the materials or to the classroom organization when he took cars from the block area to the climbing structure, or when he moved the trampoline closer to the slide. A classroom that has strict rules about keeping materials in their designated "learning centers" or "interest areas" would have seen this as rule-breaking rather than as the pursuit of meaningful ideas—as a disrespectful or noncompliant child rather than an engaged and creative learner. This kind of rule in an early childhood classroom is often implemented in the name of structure, organization, or materials management, but as we can see in this example, such a rule would have obstructed Jaden's opportunities to grow and learn.

I was presenting a workshop on schema play at a conference a few years ago and a woman who had worked with preschool-age children for many years was not convinced by this argument and insisted that it was vital for young children to learn responsible materials management and respect for the classroom. Later in the discussion, as the workshop moved ahead to other topics, the same woman lamented not being seen as a "real" teacher. This stayed with me for a few days, and I continued to reflect on what seemed to be a disconnect. She rejected the idea of free play's value, and this trajectory play story, and insisted that to be a "real" teacher, she must limit children's actions and prioritize adult goals and rules. I think this is backward. To be a professional, to be a *real* teacher of children in the early years, is to understand and accept the research and theory that points us to child-led play, and to be informed by children's development in all domains, not just in how well we train them to follow rules and participate in adult-led "structure."

SUPPORTING THE TRAJECTORY SCHEMA
IN YOUR PLAY SPACE

- Review your daily schedule. When and how often do children have time to deeply engage in their trajectory play?
- Go outside! As often as you can! Children need the space and equipment like slides, trees, swings, and space to run and jump to explore trajectory schemas. Forget everything you've been told about "taking the classroom outside" or creating an "outdoor classroom" and let them *play*.
- Have a lot of blocks, and a lot of space for block building and block knocking down. Knocking down block structures should not be immediately labeled as "misbehavior"—

children learn different things from blocks falling than they do from building with them, especially if they are driven by a trajectory schema.

- Make sure you include lots of vehicles, and a variety of surfaces and angles for children to use them on.

CHAPTER 5

The Transporting Schema

- For the fourth morning in a row, four children (4–5-year-olds) work together to rearrange tables and chairs in preparation for putting on a "show" that never actually happens.
- Three children (3-year-olds) move blankets, cushions, and dolls from other areas of the room into their new "baby space" in the corner of the dramatic play area.
- After lunch time, William (2 years old) rushes to help slide cots across the floor and into their appropriate positions.
- At pick up time, 4-year-old Samantha's mom asks her to empty her pockets, revealing a collection of counting bears and small cars.

These children are all exploring a *transporting* schema.

WHAT IS A TRANSPORTING SCHEMA?

In a transporting schema, children pick things up and carry things around. They want buckets and other containers to fill. They may just walk around the space with their hands full of seemingly random items. Children who are engaged in a transporting schema will explore in this way in multiple areas of their indoor and outdoor spaces.

TRANSPORTING STORY: BERT

Bert is 4 years old. Every morning for the last 4 days, when we go outside to play, Bert walks immediately to the storage shed to get the mesh bag full of kickballs. If all of the kickballs are already in the bag, he's ready to go! If they are loose, he spends several minutes gathering them and putting them into the bag.

Once the bag is full and the balls are collected, Bert throws the large, heavy bag over his shoulder and heads out to the playground. He doesn't play with the balls. He never takes them out of the bag. He just carries or drags them in various ways and to various spaces on the playground. He walks the perimeter, carrying the bag. He puts them on the large saucer swing and swings with the bag. He climbs the steps to the top of the slide and navigates changes in the space—the slide, a tunnel, other children.

One morning, the bag of balls was a bag of dinosaur eggs. This didn't change the way Bert carried or dragged the bag, just the way he talked about what he was carrying. This was the only day that he labeled his transporting props—every other day we saw this play it was just a bag of kickballs. After these 4 days, Bert stopped this exploration.

Bert's Social Experience

It is clear that Bert has obvious trust in his environment. He knew where to find the materials he needed for his exploration. He knew he had the freedom and the ability to find and move those materials on his own. He knew he could put the bag of balls on the swing, take it up the climbing structure, and bring it down the slide with him. This all comes from his experiences.

In his time in my program, he learned that he is trusted, that the environment is predictable, and the adults are supportive. This kind of trust in the environment and the people in it is a key component for social development. If we think about the cultural focus on school readiness priorities for social development, we know that one of its priorities is group participation and compliance. A child who does not have repeated experiences of social safety over time will struggle to feel the safety necessary in school for those expectations. If we think about social development in the broader terms of living and sharing life with other people, this foundation of safety and trust is also key.

Bert's Emotional Experience

In his transporting schema with the bag of kickballs, Bert is living Erik Erikson's psychosocial theory. In this theory, Erikson describes a series of existential crises that people work through as they grow and develop. In each of these stages, Bert has to work through, with the help of his lived experiences, confusion about his personal identity. At 4 years old, Bert can be assumed to be working through the Initiative vs. Guilt stage. In this stage, Bert learns about himself as a person and as a learner based on how the world, and the people in it, respond to the ways he takes initiative to try out his ideas. In this case, we see a series of Bert's ideas about how to use the materials that interest him to play and explore. If his teachers had kept the shed locked so that only they could bring out the materials they wanted him to use, had limited the number of balls he could use, or had prohibited him from transporting the bag up the climber, he would have received very different messages about the value of his ideas and his identity.

There are mental health benefits to Bert's play, too. In a 2023 article, Peter Gray and colleagues point out the relationship between the decline of children's opportunities for independent choice making and the rise of anxiety and depression we've seen in the United States over the last several decades. Bert's ability to choose this transporting play day after day for as long as he was interested in the play, to follow his own ideas, and to take action that was meaningful to his daily life may seem like a simple thing, but the repeated experience contributes to his psychological well-being.

Bert's School Readiness Experience

Math. Bert's experience with putting the balls into the bag and having them sometimes fall out gives him important experience (and data) in a major foundational area of early math development: number sense. In *The Intentional Teacher* (2014), Ann Epstein writes that "mathematicians, researchers and practitioners agree that a central objective of early mathematics education is developing children's number sense—intuition about numbers and their magnitude, then relationships to real quantities and the kinds of operations that can be performed on them" (p. 135). There are times when Bert is filling the bag when he counts as he puts each ball into the bag, showing me that he has an understanding of the sequence of number words and of one-to-one correspondence. When he has put the fifth ball into the bag, and the last number word he used was "five," he is identifying quantity.

Literacy. When Bert moves around the playground and up into the climbing structure with the bag of balls, he has many different experiences with spatial awareness. Spatial awareness is a complex skill that helps us determine where our body is in relation to objects around us, and the position of objects in relation to each other. It's not something adults typically have to think much about, because of our age and vast experience with the concept, but for young children like Bert, it's still being learned and developed every day. As he adds the large bag to his body, it changes how he moves through space. As he learns which spaces on the climber and slide he can get the bag through (the stairway, the slide) and which he can't (the tunnel), he gains more and more experience. These experiences are vital for his future literacy learning in that good spatial awareness will help him write letters that are proportional and to space letters and words appropriately. Finally, when Bert pretends the balls are dinosaur eggs, he is engaging in symbolic thinking. The balls represent an abstract idea of eggs. Symbolic thinking is key for future reading, when he will be expected to understand that the letters on a page and the words those letters form represent an idea (the story).

Science. As he transports the bag of kickballs, Bert is showing us his natural inclination to learn about the world around him. I can't help thinking that it would be less work for him to give up and try something else each time he encounters a challenge like the opening of the bag closing up before he can maneuver the next ball into it, or the bag of balls hitting the side of the slide entryway and causing him to bounce back rather than allowing him to progress to the slide. But he doesn't give up. His drive to explore leads him to focus intently, notice what happens in these instances, and experiment with ways to solve the problem. While many school standards focus on the teaching of academic vocabulary of early science education, and early educators rely on the elaborate adult-led experiments like the ever-popular baking soda volcano, what Bert experiences here is a more authentic physical science and engineering experience.

Bert's Brain Development Experience

As Bert transports his bag of kickballs, he is moving his body in many ways, and he is receiving lots of new information about how his body moves differently when he has the full bag over his shoulder. He is experiencing how he has to change familiar ways of moving on the climbing equipment and the slide now that his body has essentially changed shape and size. The new information he gains through his repetitive play, and the ways his familiar experiences are challenged and changed through this play, can cause physiological changes to his brain as it connects the input it receives to dendrites that collect information from other neurons.

Further Discussion

This transporting exploration was completely Bert's idea, motivated by his own curiosity and drive to learn. This is important because when motivation comes from within the child and the child is allowed to act on his own interests and questions, the stage is set for deep learning, for a broad exploration that typically involves long periods of deep focus. Each time Bert transports the bag of kickballs to a new area, in a different method or for a different reason, he gets new data about the world and about himself. This iterative exploration contributes to the formation and strengthening of neural connections. Recognizing that what I was observing was a possible transporting play schema gave me a framework for making any of his "threads of thinking" (Nutbrown, 2011) visible for stakeholders concerned about school readiness, social–emotional development, or other areas of early childhood concern.

For example, kindergarten teachers and school readiness assessment tools often ask whether a child can focus on a task for a long period of time. They see a child's lack of focus on adult-initiated tasks and activities as a deficit—a "short" attention span. In Bert's play, we see the opposite. His attention and focus were captured for long periods of time each morning over the course of several days. He is given time so that he can develop habits of focus until his brain and body are more ready for the school activities that will one day demand his attention.

Additionally, he is not being asked to pay a currency he doesn't yet have (attention) for a service that does not benefit him (adult-led activities and structured direct instruction); thus, he may avoid negative messages about his identity as a learner—that if he cannot sit still, focus, stay with a group, or feign interest in what is required of him, he must be "bad" at school. He may also internalize that "school" is unpleasant. Instead, he is being given what he needs in these early experiences, therefore he will be better able to meet the needs of his teacher and his school when he gets there.

Noticing and thinking about play like Bert's transporting invites us to think about his movement needs and how his movement and thinking are connected. While the ECE field minimally recognizes the importance of movement for young children, in practice, it is too often "schoolified." The adults control the movement options and they take place as part of an overall plan at scheduled times. As Stacy Benge (2023) writes, "If they are always following movements the adults have chosen, they are not getting the movement their individual bodies need. Remember, children's brains tell their bodies what they need, and their bodies tell us" (p. 109).

Bert's transporting play allows us to see the distinct differences in lesson-planned movement activities and authentic brain/body work in early childhood. I could have seen Bert's interest in the balls on that first morning and planned kicking games or throwing activities, or invited him to roll them down the slide with me. While there is nothing wrong with those ideas, and there may be some benefit, in this approach, it is superficial. Had I stopped noticing after my initial note of his choice of material, I would be left to guess what element of the play was the most useful to my "emergent" teaching, and I would have missed all of the rich experience and practice I saw Bert engage in.

By waiting and watching, and using a schema play lens, I saw more specificity in the ways Bert used his body. I wasn't looking for data regarding his ability to kick or throw so I could check off an assessment list; I was wondering about Bert. He used his whole body to hold the opening of the bag wide enough to fill the bag. He used his torso, his shoulder, his elbow, his wrist, his waist. He crossed all three midlines—top/bottom, right/left, front/back—as he swung the bag over his shoulder. There was no dance party or Simon Says game I could have planned that would have offered this kind of depth and scope for Bert.

TRANSPORTING STORY: ZAHRA

Zahra is 3 years old and has Down syndrome. One morning, her teacher noticed her at the sensory table, watching as another child used a mallet and golf tees to chop up blocks of melting ice. Zahra walked to the dramatic play area of the classroom, found a large spoon, and carried it back to the sensory table. She began scooping up the small pieces of ice from one end of the tub and carrying them to the other end, where she would empty the spoon. She continued to transport ice from one end of the tub to the other, back and forth.

After several minutes of this play, Michael and Emmett (also 3 years old), stopped to watch what Zahra was doing with the spoon and the ice. Emmett took the spoon from Zahra and began to imitate what she had been doing—transporting the ice. Zahra went back to the dramatic play area and found a second spoon. She returned to the sensory table, where she gave the new spoon to Emmett and retrieved the spoon he had taken. They played together, Emmett imitating Zahra's transporting. Soon, Michael found his own spoon and joined in the play.

Zahra's teacher watches the play, surprised that these three children, whose play personalities are usually so different from each other's, are spending time together in the same activity. After several minutes, Michael brings a small dish from the dramatic play area to the sensory table and begins transporting ice and water around the table. Zahra notices and looks around for a new transporting method to use. She finds a set of measuring cups and begins to use them to move the water and ice.

Zahra's Social Experience

In her transporting play, Zahra is a leader for other children and in creating a community around a shared interest. Zahra usually engages in a lot of onlooker play, where she stands outside of the play action of her peers and watches what is happening. She often looks at her teachers, then back at the playing children, which her teachers believe indicates she would *like* to join the play but does not feel safe or confident enough to do so. When this happens, the teachers try to invite her to join, offer to walk with her, or ask a child from the playing group to invite her. This occasionally works, but only for a short time. Even when she has physically joined the group, she continues the onlooker play from within, rather than truly joining. This is not surprising, as Zahra's expressive language skills are not on the same developmental level as her peers. It is hard for her to keep up with them once they have started a play theme.

In the ice transportation play, however, Zahra is a social leader. It is her idea to bring the spoon from the dramatic play area and use it to move ice and water around the sensory table. *She* solves the problem when Emmett takes her spoon. As Michael and Emmett notice her good idea, and imitate her good idea, they come into *her* play. As they interact in the same space, sharing smiles and reactions, imitating each other, Zahra gets a social experience that she would not get from an attempt to include her in play initiated by adults or other children.

Zahra's Emotional Experience

Because she has a visible disability and is receiving services from many doctors, therapists, and early interventionists, Zahra is surrounded by a deficit narrative. She receives services that are important and valuable but are based almost entirely on what she is not able to do and on how she is different from her peers in the preschool classroom. In her therapies, she must participate in many activities that, while valuable to her growth, are not her idea and are not her choice. In her transporting play, she is the initiator. She has an interest, she comes up with an idea to follow the interest, she has the freedom to follow that idea, and others (Michael and Emmett) see the good idea and try it for themselves. This must have been so empowering and satisfying to Zahra! She experiences herself as a competent leader, and her sense of identity is strengthened.

Zahra's School Readiness Experience

Math. As Zahra transports the ice and water during her sensory play, she is developing early arithmetic concepts. The arithmetic that Zahra will be asked to learn in her later school experiences will build on the input she gets as she composes and decomposes the collection of ice chunks. She scoops some out of the collection and moves that smaller group to another area of her space. She sees the initially smaller new collection become larger as she transports more scoops of ice. This informal arithmetic with concrete materials will provide initial ideas that set the stage for future adding and subtracting of abstract numbers.

Literacy. Zahra's teacher noticed, as she watched her use the spoon to move the ice pieces from one area of the sensory table to others, how closely Zahra's eyes were focused on her hand and the spoon, then on the spot where she dumped the ice. This was an opportunity to see Zahra's skills at visual attention. Visual attention occurs when a child uses her eyes and body together to stay with an activity (Benge, 2023). In Zahra's transporting play schema, her visual attention helped her to see what to scoop up, to carry out her plan to scoop and to transport, and to see where she was taking her spoonfuls of ice before she emptied the spoon. This is the same visual attention that will help Zahra follow text on a page and to write words and sentences on paper.

Science. Zahra is exploring the uses of tools and technology in her play with spoons, measuring cups, and ice/water. While her teacher first noticed the deep play in the ice and water, she was able to think back to a previous (informal) observation of Zahra at snack time, when she repeatedly scooped and transported cheese crackers from the serving basket to her bowl. The use of similar tools and actions allows the teacher to see the threads of Zahra's connected thinking—her transporting schema. Zahra is showing us her purpose—to move materials from one place to another—and her ability to select and use tools to meet that purpose. This is foundational engineering in action.

Zahra's Brain Development Experience

In their 2017 white paper *Neuroscience and Learning Through Play: A Review of the Evidence,* Claire Liu and her coauthors identify iteration as a characteristic of play that can stimulate and develop the brain networks involved in learning. We see an example of this kind of repetitive experience in Zahra's transporting play. Zahra uses the same framework (moving items from one group/place to another) and the same tool (the spoon) to repeat a schema. While the play actions may seem the same, a deeper noticing of the elements of that activity shows us more complexity. Each repetition of the transporting action gives her new information—as ice stays on the spoon or falls off the spoon, as one pile of ice grows smaller as another grows larger, as one trip back and forth is undisrupted and on the next trip her arm is bumped by a peer, as she uses new tools—she notices differences and similarities, she solves problems, she practices cognitive flexibility, and her neural connections are strengthened so information can move more quickly through her brain.

Further Discussion

As Zahra's teacher watched this ice and water transportation experience unfold, she spent some time thinking about other ways she had seen Zahra play and interact with her environment that week. She remembered watching her at morning snack the day before. During that family style meal service, where the children passed a basket of cheese crackers to each other and took turns using a spoon to serve themselves, Zahra had continually reached for the basket and served herself more crackers, even though she had not eaten the crackers in her bowl. At the time, her teacher had just thought that what she was observing was a lack of impulse control or even a selfish urge to take more and more crackers. When she connected the two observations of Zahra, she was able to think differently about that snack experience. She decided that she needed to look around the space and see how many other opportunities Zahra would have to transport items in different ways.

Over the next few weeks, she made sure that there were materials that were familiar to the transporting actions she had already seen Zahra engage in (spoons and measuring cups) but wanted to invite her to extend those explorations. She added larger buckets to the sensory table, where she had first seen Zahra transporting. She then added the same types of spoons, measuring cups, and buckets to other areas of the room in the hope that Zahra would recognize the familiar tools and be curious about using them with new materials and in new spaces.

This practice of using the lens of schema play theory to support current explorations and to invite a child to apply elements of that exploration into other areas, and with other materials and peers, is an essential piece of breaking down the "practitioner attitude" barrier introduced in Chapter 2. There are two elements of an early educator's identity that can be threatened by free, child-chosen play.

The first is their identity as a "real" professional teacher. Early care and education practitioners experience a widespread lack of respect for the work they do with young children, particularly those who work in settings labeled (often derisively) as "child care." I have had friends and family members comment on how easy my job must be, "just playing" all day, every day.

Students in my early childhood education courses report to each other the responses they get when they tell people what their major is—"Oh, so you're not great at math, huh?" or "What a nice job for a young lady," for example. I have had more than one parent of a child I was caring for ask, as an attempted compliment to the ways they saw me working, if I ever considered "becoming a real teacher."

We feel the pressure to prove our professional identity—and ignoring child-led play in favor of creating practices and spaces that look like elementary school is a commonly adopted strategy. In Zahra's story, however, we see how teaching and fostering development in early childhood is different from elementary school models. Zahra's teacher had a deep understanding of how children Zahra's age typically process the world around them, how that builds knowledge, and what developmental priorities for both a 3-year-old in general, and Zahra in particular, should be. She used that knowledge to create an environment that was rich in opportunities for learning. That's professionalism. This developmentally informed and developmentally responsive approach *is* "being a real teacher."

The second is their identity as a key player in the continuity between early childhood education and elementary school. As you read in the section describing Zahra's school readiness experience, the transporting play schema that she chose, pursued, persevered in, and focused on for a long period of time connects directly to educational priorities in later school years. Her play, her ideas, and her actions can be directly connected to early learning standards in many states. Indiana's Early Learning Standards, for example, are designed to "feed" into elementary school standards. Rather than trying to engage Zahra in adult-led, kindergarten/1st-grade tasks at an earlier age, as some do when striving for this continuity, we see Zahra's teacher able to recognize the foundational value of her current experiences and potential learning. We are able to look at the schema play and match it to age-appropriate standards to make that learning visible to other stakeholders, and to use the language of learning standards to make our case for Zahra's play. For example, using the Indiana Early Learning Standards (Indiana Department of Education, 2023), in this play we see Zahra practicing M2.1 "Exhibit understanding of mathematical structure." When Zahra brings new materials to the play, or notices other children joining or leaving the play, she is identifying "that an object has been added to a group," which is a key experience for understanding that "numbers can be composed and decomposed to create new numbers" (p. 12).

SUPPORTING THE TRANSPORTING SCHEMA
IN YOUR PLAY SPACE

- Find elements in your daily routines where children's transporting schema can be included. For example, family-style meal service where children can pass serving bowls, giving children totes to carry diapering and toileting items, allowing children to help move cots or nap mats, or providing wagons or tubs with handles to use during clean up times.

- Reflect on your thinking about children's behavior regarding transporting. It may appear that a child is being "sneaky" or trying to steal/hide small toys when they transport them in their pockets or hands.
- Do you have rules that limit the learning that could be taking place with a transporting schema? Some early childhood practitioners set limits like not allowing items from one learning center/classroom area to be taken to another area, like not allowing sand out of the sand area, saying books have to stay in the book corner or blocks can't be taken into dramatic play. While it may be easier to try and keep the space organized in these ways, limiting exploration limits learning.
- Make sure you have lots of items to carry and lots of ways to carry them! Add buckets, pulleys, wheeled toys, baskets, purses, wagons, and other "containers."

CHAPTER 6

The Rotation and Circularity Schema

- When umbrellas are introduced as a "loose part" for play, several of the 3- and 4-year-old children open them and try spinning them in the air in front of them or on the floor.
- After reading *Chicka Chicka Boom Boom*, coconuts are added to the indoor bowling set in place of the plastic bowling balls. Three-year-old Annie tries repeatedly to get the coconut to roll straight, but it always rolls off to the side and stops. She finds other balls to use and has better success. When another child struggles in the same way with the coconut, Annie offers the ball.
- Four-year-olds Caleb and Abel make snow angels on the playground, standing up each time to look at the arc pattern their arms and legs make. Caleb wants a "bigger circle," so they lie back down and try to spin their whole bodies instead of just their arms and legs.

These children are exploring the *rotation and circularity* schema.

WHAT IS A ROTATION AND CIRCULARITY SCHEMA?

Children exploring rotation and circularity are interested in things that turn and spin, but also in exploring curved lines and arcs. They may be drawn to wheeled vehicles, materials with screw-top lids or water wheels. They may move their hands in circles while fingerpainting or draw curved lines in their mark making. They spin their bodies in circles or enjoy pushing others on the merry-go-round. They may want to roll down hills or twist the ropes of their swing to let it spin them until they are untwisted.

ROTATION AND CIRCULARITY STORY: ELIJAH

Elijah is a 4-year-old boy who attends preschool three mornings a week. He has not been officially diagnosed with any developmental disorders or language delays, but his parents are concerned about his social skills and his repetitive play. They worry because when given the choice, even when there are several peers and numerous options at preschool, he plays alone and usually only with cars. At the preschool, there is a large yellow dump truck that is his favorite. We certainly see the preference— the desire to play only with this truck, and primarily away from other children. His parents have requested that we not allow him to play with the truck. They ask if we can remove it from the classroom.

Because we follow a free play pedagogy in our classroom, I am hesitant to put this absolute limit on Elijah's play. After a couple of conversations with his parents, I begin to wonder if I have been missing something in my observations of Elijah. I begin to wonder about the rotation and circulation schema. Was it possible that the appeal of the dump truck in the preschool, and with other cars and trucks at home, was with the turning of the wheels?

I looked around our classroom to see where else we could add elements of rotation and circularity. We added paint rollers to the art area, as well as adding small cars to the tray of the easel for driving though paint. We added a grocery cart and a stroller to our dramatic play area. We added water wheels to the water play table.

While the dump truck continued to be Elijah's favorite, we saw him venture out into the other areas where we had added things that rolled and turned. He loved painting at the easel with the cars, when we had never seen him choose art before! When he used the grocery cart in the dramatic play area, we saw him first watch other children engage together in pretend play and slowly join in when the ideas they were trying interested him. We saw Elijah try new things without having to deprive him of the toy that interested him the most.

Elijah's Social Experience

Elijah's consistent choice to play with the truck on his own did not provide him with many opportunities to interact with other children. Self-regulation, a social skill that just begins to develop during these early years, depends on a child being able to see and to try effective strategies for interacting with other children, and Elijah was not pursuing these kinds of opportunities. When the grocery cart and stroller (and their wheels) were added to the dramatic play area, the environment now invited him to explore his interest in wheels in a space where other children were pretending, talking, and playing together.

While some consider this "onlooker" stage of play to be more appropriate for a toddler than a child Elijah's age, watching others play holds a lot of developmental social value and is not indicative of any sort of delayed development. As he watches, he hears the other children talk out their pretend play scenarios. He plays with the stroller and grocery cart, which keeps him in the dramatic play area and allows him to see and hear that each child has their own ideas and perspective about the play. This emergent perspective-taking is key to most of the other social skills Elijah is developing.

Elijah's Emotional Experience

In their book, *Supporting Young Children to Cope, Build Resilience, and Heal from Trauma Through Play: A Guide for Early Childhood Educators* (2023), Nicholson et al. write, "When children bring their thoughts, feelings, and questions into play, they have the opportunity of a felt sense of being in control, even though the reality for young children is that they rarely do have control over their circumstances and schedules that dictate their daily lives" (p. 30). Elijah's story began with adult concern about the way he was choosing to play but ended with his experience of being seen and valued—instead of judging and deciding, the adults wondered about his thoughts, feelings, and questions, and tested their hypothesis that he was fascinated by rotation. Many typical preschool programs fill their schedules with the adults' timelines, thoughts, feelings, and questions and leave very little room for the child to feel that they have any agency over what happens to them. This lack of internal locus of control can negatively impact a child's mental health. When Elijah repeatedly experiences the felt sense of being in control described by Nicholson and her coauthors, he is given an opportunity to develop a kind of cushion against stress, anxiety, and depression.

Elijah's School Readiness Experience

Math. In their book, *Loose Parts: Inspiring Play in Young Children* (2014), Daly and Beloglovsky write that "being able to make a comparison provides understanding between the parts of a whole. When children take an item and compare it to another item, they gain knowledge of how things work—how they are the same, different." Although Elijah's rotation schema play is not specifically centered on loose parts material, his experience is similar and provides similar practice. Noticing similarities and differences is a key skill for mathematics, as it contributes to his ability to match, sort, and solve problems. As Elijah observes the ways the wheels in his various play experiences rotate in the same ways, but also present differences in size, speed, effect, and appearance, he is preparing for basic arithmetic and number operations (he will need to be able to compare quantities and sizes to count, add, subtract) and put objects in order based on their characteristics (such as length or weight, for example)—all of which require that he notice details that match or do not match. Additionally, noticing characteristics of the truck's wheels and remembering them as he mentally compares them to the characteristics of the paint roller offer practice with memory, a key skill in a variety of mathematical problem solving.

Literacy. It is well established that pretend play experiences in early childhood develop two key skills for future reading: symbolic representation and language acquisition. If we had not noticed Elijah's interest in rotation and supported the interest by adding more materials that had rotating parts, he may not have been drawn to the dramatic play area. His preference was playing with one truck, in a space big enough to push it around. When the grocery cart and stroller were added to the dramatic play area, so was Elijah! So, even though this would not have been written on a typical early childhood classroom's lesson plan as a "literacy" activity, it is strengthening these two foundational skills.

Elijah was introduced to new language and vocabulary as he first watched the others in their pretend play and then began to enter the play and use his expressive language. This also contributed to his contextual awareness—the ability to use information from the play to understand the story being played out and to add his own ideas to the pretend scenario. Both elements of language development are key to reading comprehension.

He experienced other children modeling symbolic representation and eventually began to follow their lead. As an empty plate became full of pretend food for a baby doll, as he connected the plastic yellow grocery cart to the large gray grocery carts that he had seen in real grocery stores, and as he used a rectangular wooden block as a telephone to call the baby's mom, he used objects to represent his ideas and to extend his play. When he starts formal reading instruction, this will be an important skill—he will need to understand that the marks on the page represent words, that words are made up of smaller marks that represent sounds, and that the written words represent stories or instructions. If we had simply taken the truck out of the room without reflecting on why the truck was so interesting and/or engaged in teacher research by adding more wheels around the room, Elijah may have not been as actively engaged in this pretending.

Science. The observable, repeated patterns of schema play capture the essence of emerging scientific thinking—looking closely at similarities and differences, at patterns and change. Without this skill, it would be difficult to identify problems, hypothesize about what might happen with different experiments, and apply past knowledge to new problems. When Elijah expands his play from solitary play with one specific truck into different areas of the room, different people to interact with, and different materials that share the similarity of rotation, his opportunity for noticing a broader set of data about things that rotate and what he can do with them is build upon his scientific literacy. He collects information from each different rotation experience and must decide which data fit into his existing experiences, which data are new, and how new data might challenge existing knowledge. Learning what is similar to other rotation play and what is different offers Elijah the chance to make predictions about future rotation play. Predicting is a key science skill.

Elijah's Brain Development Experience

Spontaneous movement is crucial to the formation of neural pathways as the brain grows and expands in the first five years of life (O'Connor & Daly, 2016), and Elijah is moving his body in a variety of ways as he explores all of the rotation contexts that the environment offers him. If the idea that more brain development happens in the first 3 to 5 years than at any other time of life had been interpreted as "We need to include as much teacher-led academic training as possible," instead of acknowledging that play and movement are the primary pathways to brain growth, Elijah would have lost this opportunity.

Once the neural connections are formed, it's important that he is provided with an environment that will contribute to myelination, which is the formation of a fatty coating around the axon that acts as an insulator that increases the speed at which signals travel through the brain circuitry, by allowing time and space for repeating these movements and experiences.

Further Discussion

We cannot erase the value of movement and physical development in our misguided focus on *readiness* and the direct instruction of academic content in early childhood settings. In Elijah's schema play, he is in constant motion regardless of which rotating materials he is using. In his play, he is moving in ways that will link his body with his brain. O'Connor and Daly (2016) remind us, "It's the voluntary movement that matters." Neuroscience should inform our decisions about what kinds of learning we value and expectations we have for children and their bodies. Cognition (development of mental processes), memory, and motivation are learned, practiced, and perfected through physical activity, not by sitting crisscross applesauce and passively listening to a teacher, or through long periods of sitting at tables or desks, or by completing worksheets or other projects that have been chosen for children by adults, for adult goals.

It's also important to acknowledge in this discussion that one of the reasons Elijah's parents wanted us to take his preferred truck out of our classroom was because he exclusively played with this one truck, and they were worried about autism and the negative interpretations of autistic play. Repetitive play or "obsessive interest" in specific materials is often included on "indicator" lists for autism. Individualized education plans (IEPs) for autistic children often include goals focused on changing the way the child chooses to play in favor of types of play neurotypical people are more familiar and comfortable with. Schema play theory helped us navigate this, as I was deeply uncomfortable with judging Elijah's choice in this way, or "tricking" him by removing his preferred object. It started when I wondered if it was the rotation of the tires that drew him to the truck and seemed to be confirmed by the way he branched out into other types of play that also fit that schema. He still had his preferred truck and was allowed to choose it often, but also got a broader experience by moving to other areas with rotation play available. According to the definitions of play we have agreed upon in this book, it wouldn't be *play* if it wasn't Elijah's idea.

ROTATION AND CIRCULARITY STORY: MARTA

Four-year-old Marta is drawn to art experiences. She is often at the art table using mark-making materials or at the easel with paints. While most of the other children in the class paint in vertical and horizontal straight lines or focus on just covering the paper completely with paint, Marta's drawing and painting focuses almost entirely on arcs, circles, and hearts.

This morning, she is at the easel. She started with a few hearts across the top of the page and progressed into creating a large circle of painted hearts. She paints inside the heart outlines she has made and stops to look at her painting.

Inside the circle she has created from her painted hearts, she paints another circle. She turns this circle into a face by adding two round eyes and an arced mouth. She paints over the outer circle a few more times before she stops painting.

Later the same morning, she is at the art table where lengths of yarn have been cut and scattered across the table. There are also trays of paint and photocopies of the teacher's face, inviting children to dip the yarn in the paint and move the yarn to paint over the teacher's surprised face. Marta stands at the table and dips the yarn in the paint so that only the bit between her fingertips is not covered in paint. She holds the yarn at its full length over the paper, lowering it into a spiral shape on the paper. After she has made several painted spirals in this way, she takes a new piece of paper and guides the painted yarn to make arc shapes.

Marta's Social Experience

Social experiences in early childhood should be viewed beyond the common focus of prosocial behavior and compliance goals. This view contributes to the kind of tunnel vision that only values the kind of social skill instruction that focuses on group management and individual compliance, instead of considering what kinds of experiences children need for their personal social development. In this case, we see Marta being given an opportunity to have a social need met instead of an adult having their control needs met. According to Michelle Salcedo (2018), being engaged in stimulating pursuits is a basic social need for young children like Marta—pursuits that the child finds stimulating, not that an adult has decided should or might be stimulating. The only way we can know what kind of pursuits a child finds stimulating is to observe and deeply notice. When she is free to choose, Marta often gravitates to creative endeavors like painting at the easel, engaging in rotation and circularity play. She shows her teacher what her stimulating pursuit is, and together they meet her need to be accepted and recognized in her social contexts.

Marta's Emotional Experience

When we talk about *social and emotional learning* (SEL), as opposed to *emotional development*, we value adult priorities and inappropriate early learning standards over the emotional development of individual children. We try to teach about emotions rather than supporting children as they naturally experience emotions. It *is* important for children to learn the vocabulary of emotion, the way their bodies feel when experiencing different emotions, and how to start to manage emotions. However, we must be sure we understand that supporting and fostering development looks very different from didactic instruction about emotions as an academic content area. When her teacher provides an environment where she is given agency and she is provided the choice of when and what to paint, she experiences the journey of learning as a state of emotional regulation, of happiness, and of being trusted.

Marta's School Readiness Experience

Math. An element of mathematical value in Marta's play here is sort of obvious—we all love to teach and quiz children about shape recognition and naming, and she is painting shapes. I would assert that what Marta is experiencing here is a deeper encounter with shapes than what I have typically seen in an adult-led preschool setting. She is not simply told or shown a variety of shapes and then asked, "What shape is this?" She is deeply engaged with and focused on her experience with circularity. She can see, and direct, how the curves can be the same as or different from each other. She is experiencing the pieces of "arc" that make a heart different from a circle. She paints a small circle to be the head of her person, but she also creates a bigger circle, composed of individual hearts rather than a thin line around the person. This exemplifies an important consideration of the potential harm of relying on direct, rote instruction as described by Ginsburg et al. (1999, as cited in Epstein, 2014): "Rote instruction that does not emphasize understanding does little to inculcate the spirit of mathematics—learning to reason, detect patterns, make conjectures, and perceive the beauty in irregularities—and may instead result in teaching children to dislike mathematics at an earlier age than usual" (p. 132). I see the opportunity for each in Marta's exploration of circularity.

Literacy. The kind of fine motor activity we can see in Marta's painting is of course an indicator of skills that will be required for handwriting and can therefore be considered a valuable experience for her school readiness and literacy development. We also see indicators of her gross motor skills as she stands steadily for extended periods of time, first at the easel and then at the art table. This shows a level of core strength that is also required for future seated schoolwork.

We also see play elements that contribute to school expectations for letter recognition and formation. Each letter in the alphabet has a distinct appearance that is made up of straight lines and curved lines. Painting and drawing circles, hearts, people, and other shapes with arced and straight lines offers opportunities for Marta to develop the visual perception to identify and form each letter's unique shape.

Science. Marta's repetition of and experimentation with circularity using different materials is an exercise in scientific curiosity. She observes the differences and similarities and the actions she can take to create change within the structure of the circularity schema with a focus on details. While she may not be explicitly thinking to herself, "I'm noticing subtle details in all of these marks I'm making," her repeated use of arcs and circles shows us what Chris Athey called her "threads of thinking." She is actively working through disequilibrium, assimilation, and accommodation because she has been allowed to follow her curiosity. She has been given time and materials to explore the concept of curving lines in a way that allows her to observe the phenomenon deeply enough to see deeper patterns or insights into it, as a geologist does not just categorize rocks by type, but pays attention to and seeks to understand their mineral composition, structure, color, and other elements.

Marta's Brain Development Experience

Engaging in creative pursuits like painting contributes to *neuroplasticity*, which is the brain's ability to continuously adapt and reorganize based on experiences and new information. This ability will be crucial for Marta as she learns and grows. It will allow her to take in new information or changing environmental factors and respond to these changes. Plasticity is occurring more rapidly during these early years than at any other time in her life. Right now, this experience is important for her as it provides crucial input for the formation of neural connections necessary for learning new skills and for her development.

Further Discussion

Marta's circularity play is perfect for catching the attention of the adults in her classroom. Mark making in the art area and painting at the easel is easily recognizable as valuable because it fits our narrative of what school looks like. Her play matches the kinds of activities that are interesting to adults and are enthusiastically noticed and praised. Her teachers want to sit down with her, model other ways to paint and draw, suggest other elements she should add to her hearts and circles, and point it out to others who are playing in different ways—"Oh, I love the way Marta is painting! You should come paint, too!"

Marta enjoys the company, of course, and receives positive messages about her choice, her skill, and herself. That's wonderful for her! As we consider the story through the lens of exploring a rotation and circularity schema, however, we can and should go deeper than our surface recognition of painting and drawing as "school-like" and therefore comfortable. Atherton and Nutbrown (2013) wrote that one of the most important elements for children's learning, however, is a perceptive, comprehending adult who can look deeply at what draws a child to the play they choose. While praising her choices and joining her in her activity can be important, if not examined, it could be limiting. If we try to make it a "teachable moment" for other ways of painting or drawing, it interrupts Marta's flow and may cause her to lose interest—therefore losing the valuable experiences described above. A perceptive, comprehending adult who wonders about what exactly *makes* these ways of playing important for Marta can instead support Marta and give her permission to continue her pursuit of this schema by looking for details about her painting, learning about her thinking by noticing how the shapes progress or build on each other, and thinking about other ways to provide for circular mark making. A perceptive, comprehending adult can also understand that children who share Marta's interest will find and join her on their own, while those who we try to coax or who haven't made that choice for themselves may feel stigmatized or excluded.

SUPPORTING THE ROTATION AND CIRCULARITY SCHEMA IN YOUR PLAY SPACE

- Examine your outdoor space for rotation opportunities. Are there opportunities to roll? Spin freely? Are they allowed to twist the swing chains and let themselves spin as the chains untwist? Add some tires.
- Cook together. Let children stir and mix using a spoon, spatula, hand mixer, or other tools that can be "circulated" in the ingredients.
- Look at your building toys (wooden blocks, legos, duplos, magnatiles). Are their curved shapes or are they all just squares, rectangles and triangles?
- Look for round shapes or tools that can be used for painting and other mark making. Add bingo blotters, sponges, rollers, circular paper, and surfaces to paint/mark on, or balls and marbles to roll through paint.

CHAPTER 7

The Enclosing and Enveloping Schema

- Five-year-old Michael lays the still-tied collapsible tunnel on the floor and steps inside it. Then he unties it, so that it pops open, and he is completely hidden inside. He tries to walk around the room, standing up inside the tunnel.
- Four-year-old Lila creates several squares with rectangular wooden unit blocks and puts plastic farm animals inside the "fences" she's made.
- Three-year-old Taylor will only use art materials if he's allowed to lie on his stomach under the table with them.
- One-year-old Joshua sits down with a basket of pipe cleaners and methodically wraps them around his arms, one by one.

These children are exploring the *enclosing and enveloping* schema.

WHAT IS AN ENCLOSING AND ENVELOPING SCHEMA?

In the enclosing and enveloping schema, children put objects or themselves into enclosed spaces or make enclosures to put objects into. They may build forts or climb under tables and behind shelves. They may fill boxes and baskets with collections of toys and other materials. You may see them creating physical boundaries in their play, like block fences around animals. You may also see children playing with "covers"—blankets, layers of clothes, or covering paper fully with paint or other mark-making tools.

ENCLOSING AND ENVELOPING STORY: GEORGE

George is 5 years old and is one of the children who seems to have one specific schema that he repeats consistently in his play over time, rather than investigating multiple schemas. We see him explore this schema in many ways all around the classroom:

- He loves to fill the toy washing machine and dryer with clothes, taking them out and switching them over, for several minutes. It's not clear that he has a "housework" narrative. He doesn't talk about "doing laundry"; he simply fills and empties the two machines over and over.
- One of his favorite classroom materials is the basket of magnatiles. He always builds an enclosed structure of some kind, and there always must be a door that opens and shuts.
- When he plays with playdough, slime, or molding materials, he flattens it, places small toys like counting bears or marbles on top of it, and then folds the flattened material around those toys and squishes it into a ball with the toys hidden inside.
- There is a small suitcase in the classroom that George loves to fill with random materials—like plastic linking chains, counting bears, plastic dishes, cars, and scarves. It becomes a game with the adults at the end of each day, as they reset the classroom, to guess what George has closed in the suitcase.
- George paints at the easel in two ways. He paints all around the outside edge of the paper, creating a border, and then paints the full paper inside the border. He also enjoys asking a teacher to write his name on the easel paper—pointing to various spots where he would like his name written and then laughing as he paints over the name as soon as it is written.
- We often find paper from the art area, crumpled tightly into balls, and hidden in drawers around the classroom.

George's Social Experience

In *Extending Thought in Young Children: A Parent–Teacher Partnership* (2007), schema play pioneer Chris Athey explains that "one of the deficit accusations thrown at young children is that they are idiosyncratic and they 'flit' from pillar to post—however, 'flitting' is demonstrated only if the surface intent of experiencing is being analyzed" (p. 6). An understanding of schema explorations changes our assumption that a child is flitting without purpose to an understanding that they are moving through the environment, looking for ways to repeat their schema play. We see George "flitting" through several areas of the classroom. In each area, he interacts with different peers, and they connect through their shared play ideas. If George's only opportunity to "enclose" was in the block area, for example, he would play primarily in the block area, and only with the other children who primarily play in the block area. His social experience is expanded because his teachers understand that, although his play seems random, he has an intention that should be supported. The result is a greater variety of peer interactions.

George's Emotional Experience

Schema play theory highlights young children's focus on processes rather than finished products, which provides a valuable framework for George's emotional development. Children are allowed to play and explore because the adult understands that their learning and development are fostered *during the process*, not as a result of a completed product. The process is valued and permitted, so no one is hovering over George, interrupting with closed-ended questions about who does laundry at home, or surreptitiously testing his color knowledge by telling him to separate the colors before putting them in the washing machine. He is not corrected when he buries counting bears in playdough and then redirected to rolling the playdough out for cookie cutters. No one asks him "What are you making?" as he covers the easel paper with paint. He feels successful and satisfied when he is allowed to immerse himself in the process of exploring rather than facing the pressure to recreate a product (like a craft or a learning standard) that has been presented by his teachers. He is allowed to be fully in his schema exploration because instead of thinking, "This is so annoying; this is meaningless; I need to make this a teachable moment," his teachers are thinking, "Isn't George funny and interesting? I wonder why he plays in these ways? I wonder how we could extend his opportunities to play this way?" He is not subjected to the well-meaning interruptions and redirections that send a message that his ideas are not acceptable or *enough*. George absorbs the acceptance, respect, and deep noticing his teachers extend to him, and experiences himself as competent.

George's School Readiness Experience

Math. This book focuses heavily on trusting the child to show us their threads of thinking and competencies to advocate for more free play and less adult-led direct instruction. I know this may make some readers uncomfortable or defensive, or cause them to wonder what their role is in this kind of learning lens. I hope it has been well illustrated that the most important "teacher role" is to notice, wonder about, learn about, and support the child in their play. However, another role is to learn how to verbally support the play and name some of the learning they are seeing, being careful not to interrupt or turn it into a quiz.

In this case, George's teachers have an opportunity to take on this second role by modeling positional language, naming shapes and describing sizes, or "narrating" about spatial relationships as they observe his play. This kind of informal but still-valuable teaching strategy can capitalize on the joy and curiosity George brings to his math-rich schema play. As the NCTM suggested in 2022, "long before entering school, children spontaneously explore and use mathematics in play . . . and their mathematical knowledge can be complex and sophisticated" (p. 2). The task for teachers is to learn to identify it, offer support for it, and occasionally add concept vocabulary to these types of mathematical explorations.

Literacy. Each enclosing and enveloping schema experience included in George's play contributes to his future reading and writing because they each offer different types of practice with eye-hand coordination—specifically the concept of tracking. Children practice tracking when they build, push, pull, use ramps, or play with balls. I would suggest that painting at an easel is also a tracking opportunity. Stacy Benge asks in her 2023 book *The Whole Child Alphabet: How Young Children Actually Develop Literacy*, when children work with their hands, what happens to their eyes? Her answer? Their eyes typically track their hands. George is learning to use his eyes, hands, and brain together in ways that strengthen his visual tracking. He'll need this skill to follow lines of text or to scan a page for information.

Science. When George's enclosure exploration leads him to build with the magnetic building tiles, it is also supporting him as a young scientist. He isn't building for height or scale—he's building a structure specifically so that things can be put inside of it, and so that there is a door that can complete the enclosure. While the magnetic tiles have, of course, come with a book of structures to copy, in George's case, they are acting as *loose parts*. Loose parts are objects and materials that children can move, manipulate, control, and change when they play, and come with no specific set of directions (Daly & Beloglovsky, 2014). While the creators of the tiles had specific ideas about how they should be used, George's teacher's respect for free play and child choice allowed him to turn them into loose parts and follow his play schema. To complete his goal, George must translate an abstract idea from his imagination ("I want something that can hold and hide things, and a door to close them in") into a concrete structure. To do this, he must create theories of what that might look like and what materials would be best. He has to create hypotheses about which shape fits where and what kind of foundation is necessary to build high enough to fit materials inside, and he has to engage in design experiments, learning what works and adjusting what doesn't work. That's inquiry-based science.

George's Brain Development Experience

Author Carla Hannaford connects movement to brain growth in her book, *Smart Moves: Why Learning Is Not All in Your Head* (2007), saying, "Young children's future achievements are dependent on their movement experiences from the time they are born as they cause the brain to constantly transform itself in unimaginably plastic ways" (p. 13). There is movement in all of George's play, and it is a wide variety of movement experiences, engaging all of his body at different times in a way that formal movement activities do not provide. Authors O'Connor and Daly (2016) are clear that "structured movement has its place . . . but it is not driven by the same individualized programme of specific movements and relevant repetition that is triggered within each child's brain when they are allowed time and space to develop their own play" (p. 14). George's brain growth benefits from the variety of ways his body can move when he engages in enclosing and enveloping play, and he is free to repeat those movements as he repeats his play themes.

Further Discussion

George's story recalls the many people I have heard in recent years who bemoan the fact that "children just don't know how to play anymore." I usually find that they mean children don't play in ways that fit the *adult's* schema about play. They have their own mental file folders to file their observations into, and their "play folder" only includes pretend play, or sitting down to use toys that have been categorized into learning areas/interest centers at the table, or knowing how to roll out playdough and use cookie cutters. Schema play like George's, viewed in this way, would easily be interpreted by these adults as meaningless, not functional, not constructive. What a gift to have Athey's theory as an opportunity to reconsider the idea of children not knowing how to play!

The variety of ways and places that George explores his enclosing and enveloping schema might seem like meaningless, disengaged "flitting" if we are not looking below the surface. Schema play theory demands that we see children as competent enough to wonder about and support rather than dismissing play that doesn't fit our ideas of what George should be doing. He is not flitting without purpose, unable to engage or pay attention to things. He is deeply interested in the many opportunities his classroom offers to engage in enclosing and enveloping.

When I advocate for a free play pedagogy in early childhood settings, I am often asked, "But then how am I a *teacher* if they just play? How do I prove my professionalism and demand respect for my important work?" These are valid questions. I would suggest that our professionalism lies not in trying to recreate elementary school settings and expectations in programs serving children birth to age 5, but in demonstrating that we understand how children in this age range actually grow, develop, and learn. Effective teaching of young children requires that we stop focusing on performing in ways that look like school, and instead focus on how children learn, and what is most important for them to learn in these preschool years. Instead of accepting only "play with a purpose," we prioritized the question of "whose purpose?"

ENCLOSING AND ENVELOPING STORY: WARREN

Warren, 3 years old, is working hard to fit himself into a classroom shelving unit. He is focused on getting his whole body into a square-shaped section. There are several "sitting circles" (flat plastic circles that indicate where children should sit during circle time) stacked in the shelf as well, taking up about a third of the space.

He starts by sitting on the stack of circles, leaning his body forward, as the shelf is not tall enough for him to sit upright. When he is unable to bring his head or limbs into the shelf space, he comes out and sits in front of the shelf, looking at it, then looking at me with a smile.

In his next attempt, he scoots himself closer to the shelf and puts his feet in first. He works to get his hands and shoulders in the space, but realizes he needs his hands to stabilize himself on the floor behind him and the top of the shelf.

His brother and another child move closer to him, and start to cheer him on, yelling things like "Go, go!" and "Oh no! Try again!" They all laugh together as Warren falls out while trying to rearrange his body.

This time, he lies on his back and puts his feet in first. He bends his knees and continues to scoot, bends his knees, and is in! His whole body! He tumbles out, and runs to me, laughing.

His brother then tries. He has been watching for most of the process and has seen what worked and what didn't work. He imitates Warren's last attempt, feet first, and gets right in.

Warren's Social Experience

Children learn to be in relationships by *being in relationships*. The way we interact with them teaches them how to interact with others. This is one of my greatest concerns as I listen to early childhood teachers or other care providers struggle with "managing behavior." Focusing on compliance is disruptive (or preventive) of relationships. When adult interactions with children are focused mostly on direction or correction, the model for children is weakened. Warren's actions in this play might easily have been described as "misbehavior" or "not respecting his environment" by adults who don't see the value in Warren trying to climb inside a small space. We may worry about safety or whether we would appear to be in enough control of our children if someone were observing and move right to correction and frustration when Warren's need to be physically active shows itself. We can interpret his actions in a completely different light when we see it as an exploration of the enclosing and enveloping schema and connect it to a *theory* instead of as a challenge to our authority. We'll be more likely to see Warren as competent and interesting, and the way we interact with and talk to him will be different. A more positive relationship model will be reinforced for him and the peers who joined his play.

Warren's Emotional Experience

Many early childhood practitioners would have stepped in and stopped Warren from pursuing his idea of trying to fit his body into a shelf that is intended to store materials, not bodies. I suspect that the only reason he was not stopped in this instance was that I was visiting and observing, sitting near him and smiling at him as he worked on his goal. This is an example of the way we can use schema play theory to reframe children's actions. Instead of another correction or dismissal, Warren and I experienced *attunement*—as I watched and didn't stop him, I supported his individual need and demonstrated responsiveness, warmth, and even engagement with his idea and process. Attunement refers to adjusting back and forth until Warren and I seemed to be *in* tune, much like tuning a musical instrument, and a lack of attunement can cause adults to find behaviors erratic or challenging (Huber, 2023).

According to Mona Delahooke (2017), when we attune to a child's needs in real time, we are supporting the development of emotional regulation. Delahooke may have been specifically writing about emotional needs, but I am confident that this can be extended to my responsiveness to Warren's need to use his body to explore his world.

Warren's School Readiness Experience

Math. Early childhood teachers are sometimes directed to encourage peer interactions as part of mathematics teaching. The rationale for this is that children can sometimes explain mathematical ideas to their peers more effectively than adults can. Peer interactions offer opportunities for children to share ideas, explain their understandings, or change their understandings of concepts they are learning. I suspect that the folx who recommend this have in mind children at the older end of the early childhood range (kindergarten through 2nd grade) and are thinking about direct instruction. However, I think the idea can be connected to Warren's enclosure attempts and the audience of peers who watched his attempts, failures, and successes.

In early childhood, children's learning is *bodily* and *concrete*. Concepts are explored and internalized through direct experience and through the senses. In this case, Warren was experiencing mathematical concepts like size, shape, direction, and problem solving in action, using his body. He showed his understandings and shared his ideas with his peers through their sense of sight—observing Warren's exploration, then bodily, imitating his efforts.

Literacy. Oral language skills like vocabulary, attentive listening, comprehension, and storytelling are important predictors of future literacy success—and are alive and well in Warren's story. Warren tried to fit into the small space provided by the shelving unit, and his peers watched, waited, and eventually took their turns. Through it all, they were talking to each other about what was happening. They offered each other suggestions, took turns in conversation, used descriptive language to share ideas or comment on what wasn't working, and *enjoyed* the conversation.

Think about this experience in terms of the LEGO Foundation's research on learning through play. The conversation was socially interactive (How could it not be?), and the children were actively engaged in talking with each other. The experience was joyful, and so the conversations were longer, and the children stayed together longer to share their ideas. No one stopped them from the enclosure play that led to the conversation, making it an iterative experience. Imagine the benefit to their future reading experiences!

Science. Just like his math experience, Warren's science learning in this scenario is concrete and is experienced bodily. He was experiencing scientific concepts in a way that matches his development, rather than being taught abstract concepts by someone else demonstrating the concepts. For example, Indiana kindergarten standard K-2-ETS1-1 states that by the end of kindergarten, Warren should be able to "ask questions, make observations, and gather information about a situation people want to change to define a simple problem that can be solved through the development of a new or improved object or tool" (Indiana Department of Education, 2023, p. 20). In his enclosing play, Warren asks a question: Can my body fit in this space? As he tries to fit into the space, and later as he watches others try and fit into it, he makes observations about what works and what doesn't and he gathers information about what strategies can be applied to the situation. The "tool" in this case is his body. He is actively practicing the concepts his teachers will later expect him to apply orally or on paper.

Warren's Brain Development Experience

I hope by now I have been persuasive enough that you see Warren's play as a valuable experience that feeds his development and his learning. While the way he moves and actively processes information as he attempts to fit himself into this small space is certainly providing feedback that can lead to neural connections and myelination, we can also view his brain development experience in terms of his developing motivation. While some might watch Warren's enclosing play and think it is annoying or that he is misbehaving, what I see is his practice of *approach motivation*. Approach motivation involves the release of neurochemicals that tell Warren that something is about to happen that he is going to enjoy—the intrinsic achievement of accomplishing his goal and the extrinsic motivator of getting positive feedback from the other children who are watching. The Harvard Center on the Developing Child (National Scientific Council on the Developing Child, 2018) tells us that approach motivation is important for his learning and development because it leads to his deep engagement and eventual mastery. Because Warren's teacher allowed the play, and could connect it to schema play theory, this valuable brain growth will contribute to Warren's attitude about learning across other activities and school experiences.

Further Discussion

A teacher's pedagogy (what they believe about teaching and learning) informs their thinking and decision-making on almost every element of their work with children. A teacher whose pedagogy is based on beliefs that adults are the knowledge-bringers, that a successful teacher is one who can control children, and that learning only happens through experience the adult has carefully planned or during certain times of the schedule might not see Warren's enclosing play as valuable or *educational*. They might see this as misbehavior and stop it or engage in some sort of consequence for not using the classroom materials (the shelf, and the items on the shelf) appropriately.

As a young early childhood teacher, I might have fallen into this category. By the time I watched Warren's play, my pedagogy had evolved from stopping exploration like this to allowing and wondering about it. There was no safety risk; he was not damaging equipment or materials; he was actively exploring an idea and pursuing a goal. I may not have been in control of *teaching* Warren, but he was certainly *learning*.

Warren's story also provides an opportunity to think about the ways we might provide children with opportunities for big body movement without making them wait until we can go to the gym or until it's our turn to be on the playground. Young children's brains and bodies cannot always wait until the daily schedule says it's okay to move their bodies in the ways they need to. I am often asked to speak to groups about "teaching active children," and it didn't take me long to see that this request really meant "teach us how we can stop them from being so active so we can perform our teaching routines." In these conversations it is common for participants to express their frustration that they *want* to support the children's big body play but don't have space for free-for-all running and climbing. Warren's story is a good example of how young children's need to move their bodies in big ways is not always a need to run or climb and can be met in different ways if we are willing to change our expectations or definitions of misbehavior.

SUPPORTING THE ENCLOSING AND ENVELOPING SCHEMA IN YOUR PLAY SPACE

- Allow children to create spaces where they can *feel* enclosed and enveloped. Include fort-making supplies in your space, like pillows, sheets, blankets, and books or other heavy items to hold materials in place. It *is* possible to allow fort building *and* maintain appropriate supervision!
- Reflect on any rules you might have about children being under tables or in open shelves. Chances are those rules are there due to safety concerns, but is there truly a risk? As has been mentioned in other chapters, you may need to conduct a benefit-risk analysis to determine what developmental opportunities children might lose to explore this schema.
- Add lots of clothing to the dress up area! Children love to envelop themselves in new clothes, fabrics, scarves, and layers. Consider these additions through the lens of "loose parts"— are they open-ended, allowing children to use them in their own ways, or are they close-ended with obvious identities or gender stereotypes?

CHAPTER 8

The Connecting and Disconnecting Schema

- One-year-old Lucy takes a basket of bristle blocks off the shelf and empties them onto the floor. Her teacher sits down and begins to build with them, but Lucy puts several back into the basket and dumps them again.
- Five-year-old Caleb finds a roll of painter's tape on the Makers Table, along with several other loose parts materials. The teacher intended the tape to be used to connect the other materials. Caleb uses the tape to make lines on the floor, using scissors to cut the pieces into a variety of lengths.
- Four-year-olds Michael and Lila come running up to their teacher, saying, "Can't catch me!" and running away. Their teacher chases them. They stop and let her catch them. They all laugh together, then the children start to run again and repeat the chasing/catching cycle.

These children are all exploring a *connecting and disconnecting* schema.

WHAT IS A CONNECTING AND DISCONNECTING SCHEMA?

In the connecting and disconnecting schema, children will join things together, tie things up, and take things apart. They may scatter materials off tables or across the floor using their arms or legs. They may be especially interested in trains and tracks, undressing or undoing their shoes, gluing and taping materials, or cutting and tearing paper. You may notice them breaking playdough into smaller pieces and then gathering the pieces back to make it whole again. They may be exploring by building and knocking down block structures or sandcastles.

CONNECTING AND DISCONNECTING STORY: MILLIE

Three-year-old Millie has been playing with the trains and the wooden train track for two mornings in a row. I am surprised by this choice. Millie is usually found in the dramatic play area taking care of dolls and setting the table for imaginary meals.

I want to take advantage of this new interest in trains. I add train books to our bookshelf and try to engage Millie in conversation about trains when I push her on the merry-go-round or sit with her at the breakfast table. I'm surprised that, despite her choice to play with the trains, she is not interested in reading or talking about them.

Her train play continues for several mornings. I keep watching, curious about the attraction to these materials and her resistance to "train content" in other areas. I notice that when she chooses this play, she spends most of her time building the track, taking it apart, trying to build it in new directions, and working with the magnetic train cars as they either click together and fall apart or repel each other.

Millie's not playing in this way because of an interest in trains as content! She is exploring the connections and disconnections that come with these materials. Later in the day, instead of trying to talk about trains to engage her, I look for other materials that connect and disconnect, and I invite her to join me with other materials that can be joined together when she is not engaged in her own play.

Millie's Social Experience

When we think of stages and types of play as linear, and driven by chronological age, we risk seeing deficits in children who are "too old" for solitary play, but who choose to play alone. Millie's connecting and disconnecting schema play with trains and tracks is solitary, but she is not deficient, despite being older than some "ages and stages" framework ascribe to solitary play. The question arises, how could solitary play have social value? Solitary play offers Millie the opportunity to learn to enjoy her own company and her own ideas. She also can learn about personal boundaries (her own and those of the children playing around her) as they share the space and pursue their individual goals.

Millie's Emotional Experience

An important element of the connecting and disconnecting schema is figuring out how to make things stay connected and how to control the disconnection. For Millie, she must find track pieces that fit together and work out how to keep them connected as she puts them down on the floor or moves them around. She uses trial and error with the train cars, trying to find those whose magnets attract each other. All this trial and error (and success) helps Millie practice emotional regulation. She gets frustrated, she keeps trying, she has success, and the cycle continues.

Millie's School Readiness Experience

Math. Millie is playing with the train set in an open area with a lot of space, but she still must adjust when the pieces of track she is connecting start to spread into another child's play space or get too close to the wall. As I observe her playing, I can see her start to adjust as she sees the track approaching the wall. I see her look at the space between her current construction and the pieces in her hands as if she is estimating how many pieces will fit or when she will need the pieces that make a corner, to turn away from the wall. She's doing mental mathematics here—estimating, subtracting, composing, and decomposing.

Literacy. The train set and train cars are on the classroom floor, so Millie is moving from a seated position to crawling around the floor as she gathers pieces and builds further out. As she makes these positional changes and looks down at the tracks and up at her surroundings or other parts of her structure, her body and brain are working in a way that is important, strengthening the physical and visual skills she will need when she is reading and writing. As she looks to the floor, then up at her construction, and up at other areas of the space, and back to the floor, her short and long vision develop. Our literacy discourse in early childhood education focuses primarily on language development, letter recognition, and sound production. Physical development is largely ignored or not understood, but we see a valuable example here in Millie's schema play.

Science. My observation of Millie's play with the train materials changed when I noticed it was a connecting and disconnecting schema. Instead of watching and thinking about how different it was that she was choosing the train set and trying to add more train content to our classroom, I shifted to watch for connecting and disconnecting actions. When I made this shift, I watched closely how she worked with the train cars and their attached magnets. Over the course of three mornings, her actions showed me that she had started to ask questions about why it was sometimes easy to connect the cars with the magnets and why sometimes they pushed away from each other. Millie was, of course, learning about attraction and repulsion—what early childhood classroom doesn't have magnets in the science area? But beyond these two concepts, Millie was experimenting with cause and effect. What makes them stick? Why don't they always stick? And as I saw her make adjustments and try different cars, or turn cars around to try the other magnet, I saw her developing critical-thinking skills.

Millie's Brain Development Experience

The LEGO Foundation's work (Zosh et al., 2017) on neuroscience and learning through play is so important for early care and education practitioners, but also for the children we work with. We can connect Millie's schema play with the trains to all five of the key characteristics of playful experiences described in the foundation's work, but here I will focus on one: *meaningful*. Millie's play shows me what is meaningful to her—not trains in general, as I first guessed, but *connecting and disconnecting* the pieces—and by allowing her to continue to work with the train materials as she chooses, I am allowing her to connect new insights about the schema with her existing knowledge. We see this in her experimentation with repulsion and attraction and with the adjustments she makes to the length and shape of her track construction. When she makes these connections, it stimulates networks in her brain that are associated with key thinking skills like analogy and memory.

Further Discussion

My initial use of what I had observed in Millie's play—using trains and train props—came from a goal I held as an early educator to base as much of my planning as possible on the interests I saw in the children. Often referred to as "emerging curriculum," this approach is touted as being aligned with the constructivist theory of Jean Piaget, the progressive ideas of education presented by John Dewey, and Lev Vygotsky's sociocultural theory and is widely accepted as a curriculum approach aligned to how young children learn. When my addition of other train-related content (physical and conversational) to our space did not engage Millie in the ways I expected, I had to consider what I missed.

Schema play theory helped to scaffold *my* learning to account for the disconnect. Using my knowledge of schemas in children's play gave me a lens to look more deeply—my first attempt to carry out curriculum based on what I saw Millie doing was focused on the content of her play—the *noun*. Schema play theory encourages me to see the *verb*. The idea that young children are active learners who need to be engaged in their learning processes seems to be undisputed in the field of early care and education—it makes sense, then, that to truly support learning using children's interests as a starting point it demands that we look for verbs instead of nouns. Millie wasn't interested in exploring the train content I tried to add. I looked for her verbs—connecting and disconnecting.

This is a new way of thinking about an accepted practice in early childhood programs. Remember the story of the preschool teachers who noticed children using the water table more often than they had previously been using it? They noticed the change in interest and knew that using children's interests is a good way to offer opportunities for meaningful curriculum content. What did they do? They planned a unit on water conservation for a group of 5-year-olds.

To be fair, I have no idea how the children responded, whether it was truly engaging for them, and whether their interest in the water deepened. My own experience with 5-year-olds and water play would lead me to believe that it was not where the children would have gone if they had been left to explore the water in their own ways. Is there value in talking with young children about environmental care? Of course. Do I still feel like there may have been some verbs here that weren't noticed, based on the types of tools children were using in their water play? I do.

I see more "aha!" moments with early care and education practitioners and children's families when I talk to them about schema play than any other topic I share. I think this is due, in part, to the way this theory helps us to see meaning in children's actions that otherwise seem frivolous, or "just cute." It helps adults to get *beyond the cute* to the humanity behind the children's interests and choices. Author Ron Grady (2024) refers to this kind of shift as "honoring the moment" in a young child's life. It's a shift away from the tendency Grady describes as viewing "richness as something held in moments that fulfill our own ends, goals, and ideas about what early childhood needs to look like" (p. 26) to viewing moments like Millie searching for ways to connect her train cars or disconnect pieces of track when her ideas change to a moment that is rich with information and meaning.

Each of the "crowds" described in Chapter 1 and the barriers to free play pedagogy outlined in Chapter 2 are driven by the need to measure and know—what children can already do, what they are not able to do, what is most likely to show us what we have been trained by various elements to value and look hardest for—and this need to measure and show has forced us to look past children's chosen play. We want to control children's learning, so we feel we must control and lead their experiences. If we begin to connect the ways children show us what they are interested in and are able to do, what they are still wondering about, and what they have mastered as they play in their chosen ways, our responses to this pressure to measure, control, and change children can change. The result will be environments and experiences that are healthier for children and adults.

CONNECTING AND DISCONNECTING STORY: JOAN AND MISHIKA

Today the toddler room teacher is offering playdough and various props to her group of 1- and 2-year-olds. She has put out several large balls of homemade playdough and traditional props like rolling pins and cookie cutters. She has also offered popsicle sticks and large plastic buttons that are usually used in lacing activities.

Two-year-old Joan and 1-year-old Mishika each choose a large ball of the playdough. Joan pinches off several small pieces of the playdough until she has about 10 small pieces in front of her. Then she picks up the pieces and squeezes them back into one piece. Her teacher tries to show her how to roll the ball so that it is flat enough to use a cookie cutter. Joan watches, but when the playdough is given back to her, she continues to break it apart, arrange the pieces, and squish the small pieces back into one ball.

Mishika is also breaking her playdough into pieces, but instead of arranging them and then squishing them together like Joan is, she lays out her pieces and sticks a popsicle stick into each piece of playdough. She continues to explore the materials by taking the sticks out of the small pieces, and then putting them back in. She occasionally picks up a stick that holds playdough and shakes it, then puts it back on the table.

Joan's and Mishika's Social Experience

Young children, and perhaps toddlers especially, are learning how to be in relationship with others through the social interactions they have with the adults in their lives. The interaction between the teacher and Joan in this scenario, where Joan started with her playdough idea, the teacher shared her own idea, and Joan continued with her original play, is contributing to Joan's knowledge of and skill with these social interactions. The give and take we see in this story models for Joan the way two people participate in a social interaction in a positive way. While the teacher certainly was talking to Joan about rolling the playdough and using the cookie cutter, the most valuable exchange was through their actions with each other. Each offered ideas, each noticed the other's idea, and what might have been interpreted as "conflict" (the teacher rejecting Joan's idea and offering her own, Joan watching and waiting, then moving back to her idea) was experienced by Joan as a positive, accepting interaction and not as a struggle.

Joan's and Mishika's Emotional Experience

When we discuss children's physical development, we acknowledge that the body grows from the center outward. This is called *proximodistal* development. The child's development begins at the center of the body and moves outward toward the extremities. I like to think about a child's emotional development in a similar way—the child must focus on and learn about themselves before they can consistently practice consideration of others. Toddlers are often referred to as "egocentric," often with all the negative connotations that come with the word in our adult contexts. However, for toddlers like Joan and Mishika, it's developmentally necessary to focus on learning about themselves (the inner) before paying attention to other people's feelings (the outer). Of course, this is not a blanket statement—toddlers *can* show empathy and curiosity about others' emotions, but focusing on *self* is the most important task. While the context here is playdough—a common and sometimes unremarkable toddler experience—we see both Mishika and Joan able to focus on themselves and their identity. They play near each other, but focus on their own work, their own ideas, feelings, sensations, and reactions to the experience. They are building the "core" of their identity in this experience of play.

Joan's and Mishika's School Readiness Experience

Math. Before children can hold an abstract concept, they must have many experiences with the concept that can be processed directly through their senses. What we see Joan and Mishika experiencing here, mathematically speaking, is addition and subtraction. They won't quite be ready for math problems like $2+2 = 4$ for a while, but this experience with taking one ball of playdough and controlling the change from that one ball into several smaller pieces and then pushing those pieces into one again is exactly the kind of concrete math experience that sets the stage for $2+2$ or $5-3$. They physically experience more and less, bigger and smaller, parts and whole in a way that is meaningful to them with this connecting and disconnecting schema play.

Literacy. This exploration of the connecting and disconnecting schema is an example of what Stacy Benge describes in her book *The Whole Child Alphabet: How Young Children Actually Develop Literacy* (2023): "The mindset should embrace the foundational skills and recognize that if the experience develops foundational skills, it is supporting alphabet knowledge, even if it isn't an 'alphabet based' activity" (p. 27). In the same way that pulling the playdough into smaller parts and combining them back into one large part contributes to math knowledge, it also contributes to their literacy skill. What is reading? It is the understanding that language is the collection of several small parts (phonemic awareness) and that the words on the page are a collection of symbols that represent those sounds. It's composing and decomposing, and sometimes it starts with playdough.

Science. Joan and Mishika's teacher has a script for playdough play—you add rolling pins and cookie cutters, and show the children how to produce first a flat piece of dough, and then a recognizable shape from the cookie cutter. The children don't share this script. Joan focuses on the process of interacting with and exploring the playdough itself. Mishika explores the use of the popsicle sticks and the ways the sticks change the playdough.

A common early learning standard for science is to use tools to explore the physical properties of objects. In the teacher's script, those tools are provided with a projected result already determined. The children's use of the playdough, their hands, and the sticks shows they are using tools in a more open and process-oriented way. They meet elements of science standards—identifying and solving problems using tools, asking questions about properties and uses of materials, asking questions, and drawing conclusions—which is a deeper scientific inquiry than the rolling pins and cookie cutters provide.

Joan's and Mishika's Brain Development Experience

In Joan and Mishika's story, we saw the teacher try to show them a way to play with playdough that she thought was the "right" way to play. When the children persisted with their own ideas, she did not continue to try and guide the play. In doing this, the teacher offered the children a valuable gift for their brain development—time for uninterrupted play. Joan and Mishika went on to spend 30 minutes with the playdough, fully focused on their exploration of connecting and disconnecting. How often have we heard (or said) that toddlers have a short attention span? That's not true in this story. When children get to follow their own threads of thinking without adult interruptions, they have quite long attention spans. This is important for the development of their *working memory*—the ability to store and use information for short-term use. This is a skill that must be practiced for the brain to develop the cognitive processes that will strengthen it, rather than a skill we are born with or that magically appears at a certain age on a milestone chart. In this seemingly meaningless process of pulling playdough apart or sticking popsicle sticks into it, Joan and Mishika practice remembering what they have done and either do it again or try a new way of exploring, based on the short-term memories that have not been asked to suspend their thinking.

Further Discussion

It may not have been a conscious thought for Joan and Mishika's teacher, but when she tried to teach them how to use the rolling pin and cookie cutters with the playdough, she was demonstrating a deficit model of approaching our work with young children. Our unexamined practice often leads us in this direction. There is a belief that children come to us with very little knowledge and therefore we must fill them with the knowledge we have determined they need. This deficit approach to early education contributes to the devaluation of play. If we don't believe that children bring anything to the table, we inflate our own importance in their learning processes. Our assumptions of what they lack become what matter most, and we reinforce the idea that the only experiences that matter are those we can lead and measure.

The connecting and disconnecting we see in this story, and identify as a play schema, offers us an opportunity to step back and reframe. The understanding that there is meaning in this play leads us to look for the competence Joan and Mishika are demonstrating in what otherwise might be seen as merely cute or silly. This is an important step in pushing back against inappropriate academic practices that are neither developmentally informed nor developmentally responsive. Pausing to notice and wonder about children's competence and motivation is our first step toward a cultural humility that can lead us to more child-centered practices and spaces.

A 2016 book by Emily Plank, *Discovering the Culture of Childhood*, discusses this opportunity more fully. Plank invites us to consider childhood as a culture separate from adulthood in order to offer children the rich and respectful experiences they deserve. She connects this to her own experience as an American spending time in Germany, and discovering not only the ways life differed in the two cultures, but the ways her thinking had to change to exist more respectfully in the new world she found herself in.

She describes how she came to the realization that she was an "unreflective, unaware tourist" who was hovering "over a culture, visiting significant places and taking selfies in the expected locations" (p. 5). What a revelation to my thinking about working with young children!

I began to connect this idea to the traditional ways I saw adults approaching "teaching" with young children. I had a new way to think and talk about the disconnect I saw between what we know about child development and our practices in early childhood education. What if the traditional kinds of activities teachers find on Pinterest were the tourist's visit to the site everyone ticks off their bucket list, rather than a place they discovered through authentic exploration? What if my list of curriculum goals or assessment items were like a tourist's selfies at expected locations, rather than authentic experiences that are meaningful to children?

In the same way that Plank could not expect Germans to bend their practices, language, and ways of being to fit her American expectations, adults who choose to work with children must learn to exist in *their* culture and communicate in *their* languages. I invite you to consider *play* as the language Joan and Mishika are using to communicate their thoughts, questions, and discoveries. While the culture of adulthood in which the teacher existed valued the *products* that could be made with the playdough, the children were showing us unexpected sites off the beaten tourist path, discovered in the simple *process* of exploring and wondering, and communicated in their mother tongue. The job of the play advocate is to seek this cultural understanding and to translate it as needed to others in the culture of adulthood—the "crowds" listed in Chapter 1. An understanding of schema play theory can act as a guide in this process.

SUPPORTING THE CONNECTING AND DISCONNECTING SCHEMA IN YOUR PLAY SPACE

- Make sure you have lots of traditional "connecting" materials in your space, and enough for deep, focused exploration: wooden blocks, bristle blocks, things that button or zip, and string.
- Check your comfort level with "disconnecting": How do you view block towers being knocked down—as exploration and learning or as misbehavior? How would you respond to a child who is not "using the train tracks right" because they put them together then take them apart instead of building a track for the purpose of rolling trains?
- Think about glue and tape. For deep connecting and disconnecting exploration, children need a lot of glue and tape, and clear permission to use it in their own exploratory ways. Fun fact: It's my experience that children's families *love* providing single rolls of different kinds of tape and bottles of

glue once I started connecting photos of children using them in big ways to the possibilities of what the children might be learning.

- Think about question loops children pull you into—all the repetitions of "why" even after you've answered the questions. We can find ways that children use language and questions to keep us connected to them.

CHAPTER 9

The Positioning and Ordering Schema

- Three-year-old Lila lies on her stomach, under a chair, and works on a shape matching/stacking game
- Two-year-old Alejandro carefully balances measuring cups on the edge of the sand table before filling them with sand
- Four-year-old Kyle will not sit next to his teacher, who wants to read a book to him, but he moves to the window seat in the classroom and stands with one foot up on the ledge and gestures for her to come read to him there. He stands this way for the whole book.
- A group of 4- and 5-year-olds begin to dispute who should be first in line, closest to the door.

These children are exploring *positioning and ordering* schema.

WHAT IS A POSITIONING AND ORDERING SCHEMA?

When children explore positioning and ordering, they might line toys and other materials up on shelves or tables. They may sort toys and objects into categories based on their shared characteristics. It might be important for these children to have some control over food placement on plates, their position in lines with other children, or putting items in the "correct" place. They may enjoy creating and copying patterns.

POSITIONING AND ORDERING STORY: CALEB

Five-year-old Caleb has attended the preschool for 2 years, during which time he has consistently expressed a preference for playing with letters and words, and seeing his peers' names written out. To support this Caleb-initiated interest, his teachers keep a supply of index cards handy, to write out any word he requests, and have added laminated sentence strips with children's names written on them to the writing area. This area is often his first choice during free-choice time each morning. He enjoys sitting in front of the magnetic easel, sticking a name strip to the top, and using magnetic letters to copy the pattern on the sentence strip. While other children sometimes stop and watch or join, they usually move on to other choices while Caleb stays.

One day, teachers added large wooden craft sticks to various areas around the classroom for loose parts play. Caleb finds a basket full of the sticks, carries it to the writing table, and uses them to form letters he is familiar with, eventually spelling out "ha ha" and laughing as he called to us to come see what he'd made.

Caleb's Social Experience

Caleb's self-motivated interest in letters and spelling has captured the attention of all the adults working in the preschool program. It sets him apart from the other 3- to 5-year-olds, who are not showing this interest yet, or at least not as strongly as Caleb has. It charms them all—this kind of literacy is so easy to recognize and value! This is a good example of the proximal process Urie Bronfenbrenner described in his bioecological theory of development.

Bronfenbrenner moved beyond the typical focus on the individual in developmental theory and examined wider circles of influencing factors, for example, Caleb's early learning environment and the adults in that environment. Bronfenbrenner described "demand characteristics" as personal characteristics of the child that elicit responses from the environment (see Hayes et al., 2022, p. 20). In Caleb's case, his interest in playing in ways that the adults already value and easily identify as "learning" elicits positive verbal responses from his environment and adults who are eager to supply materials to support his interest. Caleb's social development is positively impacted by the relationship building that is the result of this "proximal process."

Caleb's Emotional Experience

The idea of children's approaches to learning is often considered to fall within the cognitive domain but is a great example of how intertwined young children's developmental domains are. It's not just the way that we try to make learning seem fun to children, and it's not limited to how we can motivate them into loving to participate in school instruction. Approaches to learning are connected to the child's emotional experience, which contributes to their sense of self and the development of their learner identity. As Caleb experiences the adults' interest in his letter-making, their positive response to his choice, and his own success at copying the patterns and positions that create the letters, he is experiencing a powerful sense of agency. He experiences himself as competent and skilled as he uses the tools and materials the teachers have provided because of his interests. He is living and breathing a positive approach to learning that has less to do with his cognitive skill and more to do with the way that his relationships have fed his enjoyment of an activity.

Caleb's School Readiness Experience

Math. Children's patterning understanding at 5 years old is found to predict mathematical activity at age 11, according to a 2023 blog post by Dr. Vicki Hargraves, and that's what we see with Caleb as he translates his knowledge of letter shape and formation into his play with the popsicle sticks. It may not be the kind of patterning activity that an early childhood catalog would sell us, where objects and colors are offered to children to imitate a predetermined pattern on a corresponding set of picture cards, but he is showing an ability to identify and create repeating sequences. He started by creating simple shapes with the sticks—a square, a triangle, a line. His transition into letter shapes from these basic shapes shows a developing awareness of patterning that allows him to not only recreate mental images of patterns but extend them. He is connecting the patterns he's noticed as he's played with letter magnets, tracing strips, and a variety of mark-making tools to the current tool (craft sticks) and extending the pattern by spelling something new ("ha ha" instead of the same names he repeatedly copied).

Literacy. Caleb's literacy experience may be the easiest to examine out of all the vignettes in this book—of course, his alphabet writing and name copying is an obvious experience with emerging literacy. The goal of this book, however, is not only to acknowledge and name the easily identifiable value that adults can connect to schema play, but to illustrate the more subtle ways that children's self-directed free play is supportive of the values held by the "crowds" we need to persuade. In this case, beyond the explicit literacy value of alphabet knowledge, Caleb is demonstrating a cognitive flexibility that is essential to future reading comprehension. Reading comprehension is vital not just when considering Caleb's future scores on standardized reading tests, but for all future learning.

It's often said that before 3rd grade, children *learn to read* and after 3rd grade, they *read to learn*. This is why the 3rd-grade test scores are so often held up as a standard to measure teaching success and student achievement. We know that vocabulary development and background knowledge can be tied to comprehension success and often focus direct instruction on those two elements. Comprehension is strengthened in the early years by free play. Cognitive flexibility is the ability to change behavior when changes in the environment require such a change for the child to achieve their goals. Caleb's goals are clear—to understand and imitate letter formation and word creation. His practice with creating names using models and magnetic letters as well as writing names using markers gives him background information on the shapes of letters and the pieces of each letter. When he becomes interested in using straight popsicle sticks to imitate the letters he has been writing, he must make inferences about how he needs to change his actions to meet the same goal. This flexibility is strengthened, rewarded, and repeated and can then be applied to decoding words, recalling experiences with vocabulary and background information, and applying these skills to the text he is reading.

Science. All of Caleb's letter play is an exercise in composition and decomposition, as he identifies that the whole (a peer's name) is made up of parts (individual letters) and that to recreate those letters in his own play, he must notice the pieces of each letter. When he then pursued the new idea of using the straight sticks to create letters, he moved deeper into his scientific exploration. Dietz et al. (2019) clarify this connection between Caleb's schema play and his scientific development, stating that "to decompose a problem effectively one must understand its constraints, generate potential solutions, evaluate the strengths and weaknesses of those solutions" (p. 1647). He has learned in recreating names that the letter A can have curves if in the middle of a name but is created from straight lines when it is the first letter of a name. How does this translate into "ha ha," and which version of A should he choose? Which is best suited to the tools he has? In this process, Caleb isn't merely copying the letters from a laminated sentence strip. He must develop a plan within new constraints.

Caleb's Brain Development Experience

Of course, Caleb's experiences with his schema play, his internal satisfaction, and the enthusiastic response of those around him have been enjoyable for him. He's been offered space, materials, and explicit permission to continue to follow his interests and ideas. This type of repeated positive experience has been linked to positive neural benefits like enhanced attention and working memory (Liu et al., 2017, p. 7). We often see "focus" and "attention span" included as desirable indicators of school readiness, and yet just as often, our early childhood practices contribute to fragmented attention. When children's days are often broken into 15–30-minute intervals in a rigid schedule of adult-centric activities that must be followed each day, they do not have time or freedom to develop the skill of focus or attention. When we frequently interrupt their play or the activities we have planned for them with quiz-style questions or corrections, we teach them *not* to focus. Classroom systems like timed learning center rotations discourage children from committing themselves to deep engagement and so they interact only superficially with materials, or protest the mandated transition. However, with child-led play like Caleb's positioning schema, dopamine is released, contributing to a feeling of being rewarded and wanting to deeply engage and to stay engaged. This brain experience builds Caleb's motivation to engage in activities and learn new things as he repeats and adjusts his actions. His working memory is built, and he becomes less susceptible to distractions. This experience and the resulting brain development contribute to Caleb's school readiness more effectively than our typical misdirected efforts.

Further Discussion

Much of the discussion about the value of schema play (and free play in general) in this book has focused on its value for the individual playing child, but in Caleb's story we can also see the value of his child-chosen free play for his community of peers in the preschool. When young children play together for most of their day in an early childhood program, the opportunities for each child to at some point be Vygotsky's "more knowledgeable other" abound. In this case, Caleb's interest in pursuing letters and writing, and his requests for adults to model name writing and spelling other words, positions him as the more knowledgeable other (someone who has higher understanding of a concept or increased skill), and provides a model for the peers who notice what he is doing or join him—however briefly—at the writing table or magnet board. They can observe his technical skill in holding the writing implements and copying their names with magnetic letters, but they also see his *interest in* using writing tools and learning about letters. They see him making connections between the alphabet letters they hear in songs and stories, the names they see written and posted, and how writing can be used to communicate. These are key motivators for emerging literacy in these early years. The fact that it is a peer who is modeling and pursuing these interests may make it more interesting and meaningful to other children than if a teacher had interrupted the play to lead them in a large-group activity about letters and words.

Vygotsky's work is centered in the value of play and of social interactions, and yet it is too often appropriated by adults who have taken his ideas about the more knowledgeable other to mean that only adults can be more knowledgeable—and are the only ones who can be trusted to decide which pieces of knowledge are worthy of pursuing.

Another concept from Vygotsky's work that interferes with the foundational element of play is the zone of proximal development (ZPD). The ZPD refers to the space between a child's current skill level and the level they can move toward with the support of that more knowledgeable other, and the process of "moving" the child between these levels is often referred to as *scaffolding* (Mooney, 2013, p. 101). This term has become a euphemism for adult-centric direct instruction in many early childhood conversations and settings. In early childhood education, we are skilled at euphemism—a trend I describe as "changing the name without changing our game." The more adult-directed teaching attempts are, the less likely they are to meet definitions of play provided by Stuart Brown, Peter Gray, and other play researchers. These attempts also shut down authentic social interaction. The addition of a schema play theory lens brings us back to the child and their goals, interests, pursuits, and their competence to be both learner and teacher.

Early childhood teachers often struggle to accept that children's free play is important enough to justify them scheduling large blocks of time and space for playing. I wonder if they might really be struggling with what other people will think or say if children are assumed to be "just playing." The teachers in Caleb's story were thrilled to observe, wonder about, and offer materials for his play. This is likely because the focus of his play was what Louis Hamlyn-Harris (2023) dubbed "academically traditional" and easy to defend. Caleb's play materials were writing utensils, written names, and the alphabet—easier to defend than the play discussed in previous schema scenarios. But Caleb's activity here is "just play" in the same way that Ann's and Miguel's mixture-making was. Schema play theory helps us assign value to what may be seen as valueless to the "crowds" we may be trying to persuade.

POSITIONING AND ORDERING STORY: MAX

A group of 3-, 4-, and 5-year-olds are engaging in a kind of pretend play that they have repeated every morning for several days. They are "putting on a show." However, the show never materializes. It's not even really discussed. Most of the play centers on lining up all the child-sized wooden chairs, where the "audience" will eventually sit. They discuss tickets, they make decorations, they make signs—but the primary focus is lining up and rearranging the chairs.

Five-year-old Max has been very involved in this play until this morning, when he moves in and out of the "let's put on a show" narrative to follow his own solitary ideas.

He begins to stack wooden unit blocks, building four to five blocks high, then knocking it down and rebuilding. He moves to pick up one of the scattered blocks, which has stopped near the line of audience chairs. There is a gap between a shelving unit and the last chair of the row that seems to catch Max's eye. He places the block he just picked up in the gap. He gathers all of his scattered blocks, all rectangle shaped, and stacks them on top of the first block. There is still a small gap between the block stack and the chair. He turns more rectangular blocks on their side and stacks them in this gap to fill it completely with blocks.

Max's Social Experience

It would be easy to focus on the ways Max played with the other children to prepare for their show in this discussion of his social experience. But what about him moving away from the group into his own solitary positioning play? What kind of impact might this have had on his social development? Adults are often concerned about solitary play, particularly if we subscribe to a linear idea of stages of play, believing that children move forward only in their development and only "regress" to earlier stages if there is a problem. Solitary play within that view is for much younger children, and at 5 years old, some might say that Max should have left that baby stage behind him. But learning is never linear, and framing it this way holds us in a deficit focus and blinds us to the competence children demonstrate in their play choices. Max is building his ability to be social while he plays on his own. Working on his own ideas contributes to a sense of self-confidence and self-esteem that will allow Max to be more confident in his interactions with others. Removing himself from the group to play alone when he needs to may also lessen the stress of group living, allowing him to interact more positively with others when he returns to the group.

Max's Emotional Experience

Max's positioning and ordering play provide him with *trauma-informed care*, as opposed to *trauma-responsive* care, when we know a child has experienced trauma and work after the fact to provide healing experiences. Max's play is building up protective factors that can improve his resilience from future trauma, or trauma we may not be aware of. What are the protective factors we can see in this scenario? First, we can connect his experience to having supportive relationships within a community. The teachers in this program have demonstrated that they value the children's ideas and their process. There is no pressure to "get to the show, already!" They know the process is allowing children to develop social relationships and community with each other as they work together on the tickets, the decorations, and the seating options. They see Max switch to filling in the space between the chair and the shelf with blocks, and they support the new idea with time, space, and deep noticing. He is welcome to be part of the community, but also to step away and be on his own, knowing the community is there when he is ready to move back to them.

Second, the problem-solving processes he must work through as he sees which blocks fit where and how some blocks need to be repositioned contributes to the development of coping strategies. He also practices these problem-solving strategies as he manages his emotions—is it frustrating when the blocks don't align easily? Sure, but he is motivated to move through this frustration to achieve his goal.

Third, he is in a safe environment. He knows he has time, space, permission, and adult support as he plays. This connection between Max's play and his emotional development is supported by the work of Bessel van der Kolk, whose 2015 book *The Body Keeps the Score* reminds us that "we must raise children who can safely play and learn, there can be no growth without curiosity, and no adaptability without being able to explore, through trial and error, who you are and what matters to you" (p. 352).

Max's School Readiness Experience

Math. One of the five characteristics of playful learning identified by the LEGO Foundation is that the experience is *actively engaging*. In Max's story, we see both his body and his mind are actively engaged in mathematical exploration. His body is actively engaged as he picks up blocks and reaches out with them, but he is also actively engaging with ideas as he practices using spatial visualization. He has a mental image of the shape of the block that he thinks will fill the space he is looking at and uses trial and error to try to make the block fit in that space. In doing this, he practices critical thinking (he analyzed the success of his plan based on information gained by observation), problem solving (first, by selecting which block to use, then by changing the position of the block to make it fit the space), and logical reasoning (thinking through his plan and considering important factors like size, balance, shape). These three elements of Max's block play are foundational for mathematical thinking.

Literacy. Filling the gap between the chair and the shelf with the blocks offers Max opportunities to practice differentiating figure-ground relationships. This is important practice for his future reading. In figure-ground differentiation, Max must develop the ability to discriminate a focal point (the space he's trying to fill or the individual block he is using) from the surrounding background of the busy classroom and the children nearby, who continue to move back and forth as they prepare for their show. This element of visual development is crucial to reading words on a page but is often ignored in favor of explicit letter and word instruction. If Max learns to identify letters and to sound out words in isolation but is not able to distinguish between the marks on a page and the busyness of background colors or illustrations, he may struggle to read and enjoy a book.

Science. Betty Zan and Beth Van Meeteren (2015), when writing about engineering experiences in early childhood, recommend that early childhood practitioners analyze opportunities we offer children by asking, "What is there in this activity for children to figure out?" They understood that this is key for young children to become deeply engaged in engineering experiences that help them figure out how the world works. I could have planned a block-building game or activity for the group, or just for Max, but it would not have been as valuable as this experience, where Max selected a problem to work on that is of interest to him, and therefore motivating for him. While free block building is full of invitations to design and test ideas the way that an engineer would, a new level of analysis and problem solving is presented by the boundaries of the chair and the shelving unit that challenge Max's scientific thinking in different ways.

Max's Brain Development Experience

"Block play engages the parietal lobes, responsible for spatial awareness and understanding of shapes and colors," states the author of the blog post "Neuroscience Behind the Benefits of Block Play for Children" (Better Blocks, 2024). Here is an example of a useful way to consider advances in our knowledge of the importance of brain development in the first 5 years of life—not as a justification to cram more school-like academic facts into younger children's empty brains, but as a catalyst for curiosity. Many early childhood practitioners claim to know the importance of block play, but are we curious about the elements of block play and how they connect to new discoveries in neuroscience?

Max is manipulating blocks in a way that helps strengthen neural pathways in the brain so that information can be shared between brain regions. This can strengthen Max's visual processing, so that he will be better able to interpret the world around him through his sense of sight. His positioning and ordering schema with the blocks may also be promoting synaptic growth in his motor cortex, leading to better eye-hand coordination and more precise control of his movements.

Further Discussion

Max's block play as he explored the positioning and ordering schema reminds me of the tension that sometimes exists between adult educational values and child development. Had I set out to teach Max about social skills, I might never have thought about how solitary play can prepare him to interact positively with others and would have relied on reading stories about friendship or only addressing those skills when he had made a social mistake. If I limited my curriculum planning to early learning standards in my state, I would have followed the very limited focus of identifying, labeling, and controlling emotions. My engineering instruction might have required that Max follow printed photos or patterns with his block building, and my literacy instruction might have ignored the necessary physical development of visual perception to focus solely on alphabet recognition. These limiting factors prevent us from seeing and thinking about the whole child, about foundational skills and experiences, and about the reality of what young children need from us.

Because I have the framework of schema play in mind, I noticed that Max's play seemed to fit into the positioning and ordering schema. My initial knowledge of this schema, connected with my knowledge of the benefits of block play, caused me to stop and observe what Max was doing with the blocks, what ideas he was following, what questions he was asking, and what he was motivated by. He was actively engaged in his own learning and was teaching me how to teach him through his play. It was up to me to be curious enough to connect what I already knew about typical child development for a child his age, what he was showing me about his individual development, and what I still needed to learn.

Chris Athey (2007) suggested that there is a more positive impact for the teachers as well as the child in moving away from focusing on adult-led content transmission as a pedagogy. She asserts that in programs where the focus is "one way transmission" of information, it limits the teacher's professional development opportunities" (p. 43). I agree. I might not have stretched myself to learn about all the possibilities Max was experiencing regarding academic content areas, his brain development, his resiliency skills, or his own ideas and questions had I focused too narrowly on lesson plans and presentation or content. I learned more about child development and learning because I noticed deeply what Max was doing and realized I needed to understand it better.

SUPPORTING THE POSITIONING AND ORDERING
SCHEMA IN YOUR PLAY SPACE

- Include a wide variety of collage materials in your art area. Include traditional paper types of materials but find some that are more unusual. Look around your space. What could be glued or taped to a piece of paper? What patterning materials could you add? Offer larger pieces of paper or pieces of cardboard boxes as the base for collaging, to vary the space and shapes they will be positioning.
- Create collections of small items of similar shape and size for lining up—cars, rocks, counting bears, thread spools, or plastic cups, for example.
- Reconsider conflicts about who gets to sit where or who is the line leader as a possible positioning and ordering schema exploration. Be cautious about telling children who they can and can't sit by at lunch. There's a social element to positioning and ordering schema when the materials are the children themselves.
- Allow children autonomy regarding where their food is placed on plates, or strong feelings of not wanting food to touch.
- Create collections of materials that can be sorted into categories: zoo vs. farm animals, balls of different sizes, socks, farm vehicles vs. street vehicles, etc.

CHAPTER 10

The Orientation and Perspective Schema

- Two-year-old Elaine lies on her back in the middle of the playground, looking up at the sky. As children play around her, she turns her head to follow them with her eyes.
- Three-year-old Kaden has discovered that he can see the classroom next door by lying on his stomach and looking through the small space between the floor and the temporary dividing wall.
- Five-year-old Alec uses a magnifying glass to look at pictures of animals in a book.
- Four-year-old Lila hangs upside down from the holding bar on the classroom mini-trampoline, turning her head to look around as she hangs.

These children are exploring the *orientation and perspective* schema.

WHAT IS AN ORIENTATION AND PERSPECTIVE SCHEMA?

Children exploring the orientation and perspective schema are learning about the world by finding ways to view it from different angles, positions, and perspectives. They will climb, hang upside down, crawl through tunnels or under tables, and lie on the floor. They may explore toys and materials by turning them over or around or moving them up high and then down low.

ORIENTATION AND PERSPECTIVE STORY: ALEJANDRO

Alejandro is a very verbal 2-year-old with strong ideas about what is funny to him and to the adults around him. He is having a lot of fun today because his teacher has added plain brown paper grocery bags to the space for loose parts play. Like the other children, he spends a lot of time filling and emptying the bags, but he soon has a new idea. He puts the paper bag over his head. It covers his body to just below his knees.

First, he stands still, calling out for people to look at him while he laughs. Then he starts to spin slowly. He is quiet while he spins.

He starts to try and walk while covered by the bag. He moves slowly, shuffling his feet rather than taking his usual big strides. He is still quiet, and his teacher wonders if he is thinking deeply about how different the world looks now that he can only see outside of the bottom of the bag. He keeps walking, more confidently, with full steps. He says, "My shoes are moving!" as if he doesn't usually connect how his feet are the means of his movement.

He bumps into the child-size couch in the middle of the floor. He stops, backs up a step, then walks slowly back to bump it again and laughs. He continues walking slowly around the room, bumping into things and naming them—couch, shelf, table, Ms. Heather, a beanbag.

Alejandro's Social Experience

An important aspect of social development for children is moving from egocentrism, a fundamental phase of development when the child is not yet aware that others have thoughts, beliefs, feelings, or ideas that are different from their own. As they develop *theory of mind* (the acknowledgment of and grappling with the reality that others feel and think in their own ways), empathy and perspective-taking become easier and their ability to interact and follow social norms grows. They become more skilled at interpreting and predicting the actions and expectations of others.

What does this have to do with Alejandro navigating his classroom from inside a large paper bag? Some have theorized that young children's sense of humor is connected to the development of theory of mind. In 2020, Paine et al. suggested that "the ability to conceive and express humor may be an important marker of a sophisticated appreciation and understanding of the mental states of others and of warm, intimate relationships" (p. 593). Alejandro is aware that his actions are making others laugh, and he can practice thinking about the mental states of his peers.

Alejandro's Emotional Experience

The kinds of SEL curriculum programs I mentioned in Chapter 2 that are aimed at compliance and behavior solutions, along with college courses, professional conferences, and online workshops, focus heavily on promises of developing *self-regulation* in young children. In many of these contexts, self-regulation is narrowly interpreted as "good behavior." In Alejandro's orientation and perspective play, we see opportunities for practicing a much more authentic self-regulation—learning to focus or shift attention and learning to modulate and change emotional or cognitive states or actions.

Young children learn almost everything with their bodies first, including self-regulation. Alejandro is having a lot of fun with this play, and that fun keeps him focused and motivated to continue. As he continues, he practices the flexible control of his attention, changing from what he can see, to what he feels with his feet, to what he remembers from prior experiences. His ability to truly self-regulate is developed through these physical experiences. As he moves, he monitors his behavior, controlling impulses, solving problems, and learning from errors.

Alejandro's School Readiness Experience

Math. It's worth repeating here that it is common for early educators to interpret math learning for young children as focusing solely on *arithmetic*—that is, number recognition and naming, counting, and operations like adding and subtracting. However, *mathematics* is a more accurate description of developmentally informed math in early childhood, as it involves a broader range of concepts like shapes, patterns, and spatial relationships.

Alejandro has spent many days in his toddler classroom and is very familiar with the shapes and patterns he encounters, as well as the ways his body can move through space. When he moves through the room with a large paper bag covering much of his body, he is *living* mathematics as he experiences the resulting changes. Instead of seeing whole people, furniture, and paths, he sees different and smaller pieces of each. He must mentally visualize and understand the situation from a different viewpoint. He is developing new ideas about spatial relationships. He will now have more flexible understandings of investigating new ideas and perspectives.

Literacy. Children need opportunities to develop directional awareness and laterality to become proficient readers and writers, and what better way to set this foundation than by moving their bodies? *Directional awareness* refers to Alejandro's ability to understand concepts like up, down, top, bottom, forward, backward, and, eventually, left and right. *Laterality* is the body's ability to use both left and right sides to complete tasks. It is an essential component for future literacy as he will need to be able to understand and demonstrate reading text from top to bottom and from left to right. Laterality will help him with writing when he is expected to hold paper at the same time as writing on it or use both hands to type on a keyboard.

Walking with the paper bag over him forces him to experience directionality in a more focused way. The paper bag changes what he can see, what he needs to look at, and how he moves through the room, giving his brain brand-new data about forward, backward, and down. He has to process the new way of seeing and moving more consciously due to the change in perspective he is experiencing. Changing the speed and process of moving his feet, one after the other, provides new ways of crossing his midline to build laterality. I am not, of course, suggesting that early educators should set aside time each day to force children to walk with paper bags over their heads. I am suggesting, however, that allowing Alejandro to follow his ideas, being curious enough to consider how meaningful this is to him, and learning more about how it might impact his intellectual development contribute to his literacy process.

Science. Predicting is a key scientific skill, and we see it here in Alejandro's goofy play with the paper bag. When children make predictions in their early science experiences, they move beyond random guessing and rely on prior knowledge or experiences. Alejandro is engaging an intellectual skill of anticipating what will happen based on prior experience when he slows his steps, shuffles his feet, and reaches out with a toe before proceeding. He is holding information about the layout of his classroom in his mind as he approaches the bookshelf and slows down, even though he cannot see the bookshelf. He is remembering prior experience walking into furniture and predicting that it will happen again if he does not modify his actions. He hypothesizes that shuffling his feet and taking shorter steps will give him more time to process what he can see—the floor and the bottom parts of the furniture. He is "doing science" with a paper bag over his head.

Alejandro's Brain Development Experience

Alejandro's brain is getting great practice in two key areas as he plays with the paper bag: his motor cortex and his prefrontal cortex. The motor cortex is in the frontal lobe of his brain and controls his movement. The prefrontal cortex lays a foundation for skills like planning, decision-making, and impulse control. As Alejandro moves through the classroom with the bag over him, he cannot see the once familiar space as he is accustomed to, he only sees his feet, the space around his feet, and the lower portions of the furniture and people in the room. It becomes sort of like an obstacle course for him; he must move using his body in different ways and in different directions based on new information. This movement generates neural impulses that will control the new movements. His prefrontal cortex is helping him with problem solving as he moves around the room. The problem? He doesn't want to run into furniture or people!

Further Discussion

A very common response to my advocacy for free play is that "parents want academics." My research on parental expectations as a barrier to free play supports this claim. Why do parents assume that this learning is not compatible with play? I would suggest that it is partly due to marketing efforts of toy and app creators, insisting that their products are not wasting your child's time, but are providing them with important educational opportunities. This sets up a dichotomy that play and learning cannot coexist. The cultural pressures and legislative mandates discussed in Chapter 2 also contribute to the misinformation that parents consume and have no evident reasons not to believe. Child care programs promise education to attract customers, and funding sources award money to programs that can demonstrate they are not "just playing." A national child care chain includes a photo of babies sitting in a circle, facing an adult who is holding up a book that she is reading—proof that making promises about academic success as early as infancy is believed to be a selling point for families looking for care for their children.

Chris Athey (2007) wrote that "parents who are not informed of the research basis for certain approaches to teaching may find the appearance of correctness desirable" (p. 45). In other words, if our mental model of "correct" teaching strategies is based on a school model of silent, compliant children receiving knowledge from the direct instruction of an adult, then that is how they will determine whether their child's experiences are valuable and educational. Our job as advocates is to make sure the developmental value of play is visible to parents in a way they can understand.

In Alejandro's specific story, the classroom he was in was part of a national chain of child care centers that promised children would learn. The chain sent out lesson plans developed at their headquarters, which even for 1- and 2-year-olds followed the familiar elementary school model of the adult in front of the group, doling out knowledge while children sat and watched or followed instructions for the right or wrong way to complete an activity. By sharing Alejandro's story on a "parent education" bulletin board, and displaying all the ways he was building skills in all of the developmental domains *and* academic content areas, I was able to present a different story and invite the families in our program to connect with and notice the ways that play was important for their children—more important than direct instruction models passed down from environments and expectations intended for much older children.

ORIENTATION AND PERSPECTIVE STORY: LINK

Four-year-old Link is an adventure seeker. He looks for new ways to do familiar things, or new things to do instead of the familiar things! At this point during his time in the preschool, he seems to be driven to find new perspectives and orientation. Today, he uses the large dome-shaped climbing structure on the playground.

The structure is a dome, with tunnel entrances to climb inside and various shaped holes at many levels, high and low, to look through. From the outside, the holes provide footholds for climbing.

This morning, Link runs straight to the dome, falls to his hand and knees, and crawls in and out through the tunnel openings. He zigzags, going in one opening, out the next one, etc. Then he crawls in an opening on one side, crawls across the floor of the dome, and comes out the opening opposite. He stops occasionally to stand up and look out the holes, looking out low openings and talking about the bottom of the slide and swing that are on either side, then looking out the higher openings and talking about the children he sees.

He comes out after exploring these perspectives for several minutes and climbs to the top of the dome. He asks who is inside the windows he can see in the building next to the playground. The windows are more on his level now that he is on top of the dome. He stands on his tiptoes trying to see through the windows. He slowly turns his body and talks about what he can see from the top—the cars driving down the street on the other side of the playground's brick wall, the parking garage that is opposite the office building, and the children who are now "smaller" than he is.

When he is done, he tells his teacher that he is going to jump off, but hesitates and seems afraid. She offers a compromise—she will stand next to the dome and catch him when he jumps. He is hesitant, looking first at her, then at the ground, then at her again. He jumps and she catches him.

Link's Social Experience

What would you say if I told you that Link's climbing experience was contributing to the development of empathy? It's true! Empathy refers to a person's ability to comprehend another person's feelings, to understand that other people might be feeling differently than you are, that there are perspectives other than your own. It all starts with *perspective taking*. Perspective! It's right there in the name of the schema! As Link crawls into the dome through the openings at the bottom of the structure and then looks out, he sees the playground from a different perspective—focused on the ground. He sees familiar peers from the feet up rather than as a whole on the same level as he is. As he stands at the top of the dome, he looks up into the windows of the building next to the playground and sees the people working in those offices as much smaller than they look when he is standing next to an adult. All of this is a physical experience of a concept that sets the foundation for more abstract thinking, and this is how children learn most concepts— they experience them bodily before they are skilled at using those skills mentally or unconsciously.

Link's Emotional Experience

To explore the benefits of Link's play for his emotional development in this scenario, we need to include the physical presence of his teacher as well as his teacher's understanding of schema play and philosophy regarding risk. We know that developing a positive self-identity is important for Link at the moment but will also benefit him as he continues to interact with peers and eventually with school expectations. Even though the dome is less than 5 feet high, and the playground surface is spongy and soft, climbing to the top feels risky for Link, and standing tall at the very top must have felt very rewarding! This feeling of overcoming fear is one of the benefits of risky play that Link's teacher holds as very important to his identity development. But she also knows Link well. She knew he would want to jump, but also knew that the height of the jump and the shape of the dome might be more of a hazard than a risk, so she moved closer, offering Link an alternative. Link trusts his teacher, and as he leans toward her, he experiences the combination of risk and safety—in relationship with the teacher, he is safe. His independent climbing and the feelings of overcoming fear and danger feed his developing self-identity, as does the knowledge that he can reach out for help and that he can trust the relationship he has with his teacher.

Link's School Readiness Experience

Math. What do climbing and standing at the top of a dome have to do with math? How could this possibly be preparing Link for his elementary school math experience? Kindergarten teacher Carrie Fafarman has an idea. In the 2017 book, *I'm OK!: Building Resilience through*

Physical Play, Jarrod Green quotes Fafarman as saying, "The apprehension children feel when they encounter a word they don't know how to read or an arithmetic problem they don't know how to solve is exactly the same feeling they have when they're standing on top of a big log and don't know if they can jump off. And the confidence they get in successfully jumping off that log makes them more confident in those uncertain moments with reading and math."

What is it that connects the experience of climbing high and standing on top of a structure and persisting with a difficult math problem? If Link has repeated experiences of being allowed to take a risk, and then navigating the process—learning that he took the risk and everything worked out fine, or that maybe he fell down but he survived it and was supported by adults he trusted—prepares him with the willingness to persist and the resilience to keep trying even if it's scary or doesn't work out the way he'd planned, whether he's standing on a playground dome or staring at his schoolwork.

Literacy. In a study published in 2020, Botha and Africa explored the connection between motor development and letter knowledge. One of their findings was that bilateral coordination (the ability to use both sides of the body together) improves reading skills in children. When children practice coordination of the opposite sides of their body, as Link did when he alternated his hands and feet to crawl around under the dome or to climb to the top of the dome, information is transferred between the two hemispheres of their brain. This kind of brain communication is a key foundational skill for reading—to follow lines of text across a page or from one page to the next or to move from one line to the next on a page. As the body builds up the skill of crossing the physical midline, the brain's visual system builds up the ability to cross the "midline" of a page or paragraph. Link's climbing also allows him to physically experience laterality (awareness of left and right sides of his body) and directionality (up, down, forward, backward), which are required skills for letter orientation and fluency.

Science. Link experiences basic principles of physics as he climbs and jumps. He uses his body weight to work against the force of gravity and relies on the friction between his hands, his shoes, and the surface of the dome to establish his grip and hold his place. A 2023 article by Areljung et al. describes this phenomenon as *emerging physics*, which "builds on the general idea of 'emergent learning,' that is, the idea that young children learn and experience things that are essential to understanding something that will later be formally taught" (p. 662). Link's exploration of emerging physics reminds us that many indicators of learning go unseen if we are only looking for discrete facts or skill demonstration in adult-led contexts.

Link's Brain Development Experience

Link's crawling and climbing as he explores is giving his body a workout—and benefiting his brain. This exploration clearly meets several of Stuart Brown's indicators of play as outlined in Chapter 2: It is voluntary, it is fun, it allows Link to be fully in the moment, and there is an obvious desire to repeat the experience. This is the kind of play activity that Sergio Pellis, a researcher at the University of Lethbridge in Alberta, Canada, referred to as having great value for brain growth. Pellis stated that "The experience of play changes the connections of the neurons at the front end of your brain. And without play experience, those neurons aren't changed." (Hamilton, 2014).

The front end of your brain, also known as the frontal lobe, is critical for regulating emotions, making plans, and solving problems. We see this at work in Link's climbing. He might feel excited, happy, nervous, frustrated, or afraid, and he perseveres in the climb. As he controlled his impulse to jump and waited for help, he regulated himself through that excitement and the fear that followed. During his climb, he had to plan where to put his hands and feet. He solved problems such as his foot slipping, other children climbing near him, and finding that the hole he intended to grab was too far away. Think what his brain might have missed out on if his teachers had taught him to fear climbing or that standing at the top of the dome after a successful climb was wrong!

Further Discussion

The orientation and perspective schema is one of the schemas that manifests in active, full-body exploration, as we see with Link's climbing in, around, under, through, and on top of. What sets this common climbing experience apart from another child's is the way Link communicates to us what he is noticing as he climbs. Another child might play on this same dome in similar ways but be more curious about how their body moves through space and through spaces as they climb and come back down. It takes careful noticing, developmentally informed teachers who have learned about schemas, and opportunities for both children to repeat the play over time for the adults to see those "threads of thinking" schema play points us to.

It would be easy for a teacher to notice both children playing on the climbing structure and assume they were both just active children who enjoyed climbing and needed to "get their wiggles out," and that letting them do so would result in quieter, more compliant children who would be ready to sit and learn when they return to the classroom. This teacher would miss out on all the *meaningful, iterative, joyful, actively engaging* learning that was already happening, in different ways for both children as they used the same structure and verb. Active physical play is often ignored as valuable to children's development and learning and is seen only as a barrier to teaching (when the moving happens at the wrong times) or a tactic (letting them be active at select times so that you can gain control for your goals). But Link in his perspective exploration and the hypothetical peer with their trajectory exploration are both actively growing in all developmental domains as they play, in a way that could not be replicated, predicted, or standardized in line with traditional curriculum practices. As Atherton and Nutbrown (2013) explain, "the extent to which adults respond to children's thinking depends on their own professional knowledge, skills, and understanding" (p. 23). The schema play framework can offer encouragement to notice, pause, wonder, and learn more to support the whole child and their learning.

SUPPORTING THE ORIENTATION AND PERSPECTIVE SCHEMA IN YOUR PLAY SPACE

- Make sure your space includes items to look through that might change what children can see—cardboard tubes, magnifying glasses, binoculars, sunglasses, and colored cling wrap on windows.
- Consider any discomfort with children taking risks like climbing, jumping, or hanging upside down. If you are worried, move closer to the child before deciding their exploration is not okay. Talk with a coworker who is more comfortable and develop a tag-team approach—call them over to be the risk supervisor!
- Include lots of mirrors in a variety of interesting places so children can see themselves from different perspectives— mirrors on walls, the floor, various heights on the wall, and the ceiling.
- Take photos of familiar classroom materials from an "aerial" view and create books, poster boards, or matching games using these photos that show new perspectives.

Conclusion

Children need to play, and play is disappearing from their lives. We can help. We create and contribute to the systems that are erasing play, and that means we can create and contribute to better systems, systems that support play and make the value of play visible to others. They can then join our efforts, and we become even more effective in bringing free play back to children. Schema play theory provides a framework for these advocacy efforts. We learn about schema play and then we start to see it. Each schema play story becomes a tool for persuading play skeptics.

You want to let them play, but the mom from the parent crowd worries that her child will fall behind her nephew whose child care program sends him home with worksheets? You can tell her stories like Bert's, whose pretend play with the bag of kickballs built the symbolic thinking skills he needed to become a strong reader, and whose practice with spatial awareness prepared him for writing his name on a piece of paper.

You want to let them play, but your center director is a member of the SEL crowd, worried that disruptive behavior is preventing children from learning? You can tell them the story of Ann, whose leadership skills were clear in her play and helped you break away from labeling her as bossy and in need of social skills training. Or the story of Jaden, who built his resiliency skills when he persisted through trial and error and more trial and error to achieve his goal of rolling the car down the pool noodle.

You want to let them play, but you've spent your whole career in the playing teacher crowd and you don't want to lose your identity as a "real teacher?" Reread the story of Millie, whose play with the train tracks helped her develop her mathematical thinking.

You want to let them play, but your early childhood education professor was a card-carrying member of the STEM crowd and only presented you with practice and instruction related to explicit, direct instruction of science concepts? Think about Warren, and how he used his body as a tool to test his hypothesis that he could fit into the space in the shelving unit.

You want to let them play, but the special guest on your favorite education podcast hails from the neuroscience crowd and has you worried that if you don't focus enough on academic content, the brains of the children in your class won't meet their full potential? Think about how George's constant and varied movement around the room, and then up and down off the floor as he enclosed and enveloped provided him with the kind of movement and sensory input that *truly* builds a brain.

Start collecting your own stories.

And let them play.

References

Areljung, S., Bäckström, L., & Grenemark, E. (2023). Young children's learning in physics: A (dis-)trustful play with gravity, friction and counterforces? *European Early Childhood Education Research Journal, 31*(4), 660–672. https://doi.org/10.1080/1350293x.2023.2177320

Atherton, F., & Nutbrown, C. (2013). *Understanding schemas and young children*. SAGE.

Athey, C. (2007). *Extending thought in young children: A parent–teacher partnership*. SAGE.

Benge, M.S.S. (2023). *The whole child alphabet: How young children actually develop literacy*. Exchange Press.

Better Blocks. (2024). *The neuroscience behind the benefits of block play for children*. https://better-blocks.com/the-neuroscience-behind-the-benefits-of-block-play-for-children

Botha, S., & Africa, E. K. (2020). The effect of a perceptual-motor intervention on the relationship between motor proficiency and letter knowledge. *Early Childhood Education Journal, 48*, 727–737. https://doi.org/10.1007/s10643-020-01034-8

Brierley, J. (2018). Are we underestimating 2 year olds? Recognizing the links between schema and mark making, implications for future pedagogy. *Journal of Early Childhood Research, 16*(2), 136–147.

Brown, S. (2009). *Play: How it shapes the brain, opens the imagination and invigorates the soul*. Penguin.

Burkins, J., & Yates, K. (2021). *Shifting the balance: 6 Ways to bring the science of reading into the balanced literacy classroom*. Stenhouse Publishers.

Christakis, E. (2017). *The importance of being little: What young children really need from grown ups*. Penguin.

Conkbayir, M. (2017). *Early childhood and neuroscience: Theory, research and implications for practice*. Bloomsbury Academic.

Connell, G., & McCarthy, C. (2013). *A moving child is a learning child: How the body teaches the brain to think (birth to age 7)*. Free Spirit Publishing.

Daly, L., & Beloglovsky, M. (2014). *Loose parts: Inspiring play in young children*. Redleaf Press.

Delahooke, M. (2017). *Social and emotional development in early intervention*. PESI Publishing & Media.

Dietz, G., Landay, J. A., & Gweon, H. (2019). Building blocks of computational thinking: Young children's developing capacities for problem decomposition. *Proceedings of the Annual Meeting of the Cognitive Science Society, 41.* https://escholarship.org/uc/item/5tt891kg

Epstein, A. S. (2014). *The intentional teacher: Choosing the best strategies for young children's learning.* Conran Octopus.

Farran, D. C. (2022, February 12). *Early developmental competencies: Or why pre-K doesn't have lasting effects.* DEY Defending the Early Years. https://dey.org/early-developmental-competencies-or-why-pre-k-does-not-have-lasting-effects

Featherstone, S. (2017). *An anthology of educational thinkers: Putting theory into practice in the early years.* Featherstone.

Ginsburg, H. P., Inoue, N. & Seo, K. H. (1999). "Young children doing mathematics: Observations of everyday activities." In J. V. Copley (Ed.), *Mathematics in the Early Years* (pp. 88–99). National Council of Teachers of Mathematics; NAEYC.

Ginsburg, K. R., the Committee on Communications, & the Committee on Psychosocial Aspects of Child and Family Health. (2007). The importance of play in promoting healthy children development and maintaining strong parent-child bonds. *American Academy of Pediatrics, 119*(1), 182–191. https://doi.org/10.1542/peds.2006-2697

Grady, R. (2024). *Honoring the moment in young children's lives: Observation, documentation, and reflection.* Redleaf Press.

Gray, P. (2011). The decline of play and the rise of psychopathology in children and adolescents. *American Journal of Play, 3*(4), 443–463.

Gray, P., Lancy, D. F., & Bjorklund, D. F. (2023). Decline in independent activity as a cause of decline in children's mental well-being: Summary of the evidence. *The Journal of Pediatrics, 260,* 113352. https://doi.org/10.1016/j.jpeds.2023.02.004

Green, J. (2017). *I'm OK!: Building resilience through physical play.* Redleaf Press.

Grimmer, T. (2017). *Observing and developing schematic behaviour in young children: A professional's guide for supporting children's learning, play and development.* Jessica Kingsley Publishers.

Hamilton, J. (2014, August 6). *Scientists say child's play helps build a better brain.* NPR. https://www.npr.org/sections/ed/2014/08/06/336361277/scientists-say-childs-play-helps-build-a-better-brain

Hamlyn-Harris, L. (2023). One center, two programs: Finding promise within a fragmented and unequal non-system. In M. K. Nagasawa, L. Peters, M. N. Bloch, & B. B. Swadener (Eds.), *Transforming early years policy in the U.S.: A call to action* (pp. 19–24). Teachers College Press.

Hannaford, C. (2007). *Smart moves: Why learning is not all in your head* (2nd ed.). Great Ocean Publishers.

Hargraves, V. (2023 May 5). The role of pattern in young children's early mathematical thinking. *Education Hub.* https://theeducationhub.org.nz/the-role-of-pattern-in-childrens-early-mathematical-understanding/

Hayes, N., O'Toole, L., & Halpenny, A. M. (2023). *Introducing Bronfenbrenner: A guide for practitioners and students in early years education.* Routledge.

Hirsh-Pasek, K., Golinkoff, R. M., Berk, L. E., & Singer, D. G. (2009). *A mandate for playful learning in preschool: Presenting the evidence.* Oxford University Press.

Howard, J. (2010). Early years practitioners' perceptions of play: An exploration of theoretical understanding, planning and involvement, confidence and barriers to practice. *Educational & Child Psychology, 27*(4), 91–102.

Huber, M. (2023). *Inclusion includes us: Building bridges and removing barriers in early childhood classrooms.* Redleaf Press.

Indiana Department of Education. (2023). *Indiana early learning standards.* https://media.doe.in.gov/news/2023-early-learning-standards-final-5-25-23.pdf

International Play Association-USA. (n.d.). *What is Article 31?* IPA-USA. https://ipausa.org/advocacy/what-is-article-31

Jacobs, N. L. & Eskridge, B. J. (1999). Teacher memories: Support or hindrance to best practice?. *Young Children, 54*(5), pp 64–67.

Jacobson, L. (2018). *How filmmaker Rob Reiner put early childhood in the limelight. K–12 Dive.* https://www.k12dive.com/news/how-filmmaker-rob-reiner-put-early-childhood-in-the-limelight/532643/

Kane, N. (2016). The play-learning binary: U.S. parents' perceptions on preschool play in a neoliberal age. *Children in Society, 30,* 290–301.

Keskin, B. (2018). The myth of the well-known "solution" of push-down academics. *Journal of Family Strengths, 18*(1), 1–9.

Landreth, G. L. (2023). *Play therapy: The art of the relationship* (4th ed.). Brunner-Routledge.

Lemay, L., Bigras, N., & Bouchard, C. (2016). Respecting but not sustaining play: Early childhood educators' and home childcare providers' practices that support children's play. *Early Years: An International Research Journal, 36*(4), 383–398.

Liu, C., Solis, L., Jensen, H., Hopkins, E., Neale, D., Zosh, J., Hirsh-Patek, K., & Whitebread, D. (2017). *Neuroscience and learning through play: A review of the evidence.* The LEGO Foundation. https://akcesedukacja.pl/images/dokumenty-pdf/Insight_and_Research/LEGO-Foundation---Neuroscience-and-learning-through-play-2017.pdf

Louis, S., Beswick, C., & Featherstone, S. (2013). *Understanding schemas in young children: Again! Again!* A&C Black.

Mooney, C. G. (2013). *Theories of childhood: Introduction to Dewey, Montessori, Erikson, Piaget, and Vygotsky.* Redleaf Press.

Morgan, A. (2019). *The paradox of sitting still in preschool.* Not Just Cute. Retrieved June 24, 2023, from https://notjustcute.com/2019/03/27/the-paradox-of-sitting-still-in-preschool/

NAEYC National Governing Board. (2019). *Professional standards and competencies for early childhood educators.* National Association for the Education of Young Children. https://www.naeyc.org/sites/default/files/globally-shared/downloads/PDFs/resources/position-statements/standards_and_competencies_ps.pdf

National Council of Teachers of Mathematics [NCTM]. (2022, November). *Mathematics in early childhood learning.* https://www.nctm.org/standards

-and-positions/position-statements/mathematics-in-early-childhood
-learning

National Scientific Council on the Developing Child. (2018). *Understanding motivation: Building the brain architecture that supports learning, health, and community participation.* Center on the Developing Child at Harvard University. https://developingchild.harvard.edu/resources/working-paper/understanding-motivation-building-the-brain-architecture-that-supports-learning-health-and-community-participation/

Nicholson, J., Kurtz, J., Edwards, L., Iris-Wilbanks, J., Watson-Alvarado, S., Jevgjovikj, M., & Torres, V. (2023). *Supporting young children to cope, build resilience, and heal from trauma through play: A practical guide for early childhood educators.* Routledge.

Nutbrown, C. (2011). *Threads of thinking: Schemas and young children's learning.* SAGE Publications.

O'Connor, A., & Daly, A. (2016). *Understanding physical development in the early years: Linking bodies and minds.* Routledge.

Paine, A. L., Karajian, G., Hashmi, S., Persram, R. J., & Howe, N. (2020). "Where's your bum brain?" Humor, social understanding, and sibling relationship quality in early childhood. *Social Development, 30*(2), 592–611. https://doi.org/10.1111/sode.12488

Pierson, A. (2018, January 29). *Exploring state-by-state definitions of kindergarten readiness to support informed policymaking.* Regional Education Laboratory Program Northwest. Retrieved April 6, 2023, from https://ies.ed.gov/learn/blog/exploring-state-state-definitions-kindergarten-readiness-support-informed-policymaking

Plank, E. (2016). *Discovering the culture of childhood.* Redleaf Press.

Salcedo, M. (2018). *Uncover the roots of challenging behavior: Create response environment where young children thrive.* Free Spirit Publishing.

van der Kolk, B. A. (2015). *The body keeps the score: Brain, mind, and body in the healing of trauma.* Penguin Books.

Wen, X., Elicker, J. G., & McMullen, M. B. (2011). Early childhood teachers' curriculum beliefs: Are they consistent with observed early classroom practices? *Early Education and Development, 22*(6), 945–969.

Yogman, M., Garner, A., Hutchinson, J, Hirsh-Pasek, K., & Golinkoff, R. M. (2018). The power of play: A pediatric role in enhancing development in young children. *Pediatrics, 142*(3), e20182058. https://pediatrics.aappublications.org/content/142/3/e20182058

Zan, B., & Van Meeteren, B. (2015). *Problem solving: Engineering experiences in early childhood.* Commuity Playthings. https://www.communityplaythings.com/resources/articles/engineering-experiences-in-early-childhood

Zosh, J. M., Hopkins, E. J., Jensen, H., Liu, C., Neale, D., Hirsh-Pasek, K., Solis, S. L., & Whitebread, D. (2017). *Learning through play: a review of the evidence* [White paper]. The LEGO Foundation.

Index

About the Author

For 35 years, Heather Bernt-Santy has been living her commitment to children, their families, and their teachers. You may know Heather from her work as the host of the internationally popular early care and education podcast *That Early Childhood Nerd*, but she also loves her work as a speaker, consultant, writer, and professor. She has held just about every position possible in the field of early care and education: teacher, director, family child care provider, education director—you name it, she's probably tried it! Heather is an enthusiastic believer in children's right to play and in the research that tells us *play* is *right*.